Desserts and Candy

Includes Crockery and Microwave Instructions

HOME COOKING LIBRARY

Banner Press • New York

It's Smart To Be Careful 5
Home Cooking In The Microwave Oven 8
Home Cooking In The Slow Cooker 10
Desserts 11
Candies And Confections 48
Measurements And Equivalents
.... inside back cover

There's No Substitute for Accuracy

Read recipe carefully.

Assemble all ingredients and utensils.

Select pans of proper kind and size. Measure pans inside, from rim to rim.

Use standard measuring cups and spoons. Use liquid measuring cups (rim above 1-cup line) for liquids. Use nested or dry measuring cups (1-cup line even with top) for dry ingredients.

Check liquid measurements at eye level.

Level dry measurements with straight-edged knife or spatula.

Sift all flour except whole-grain types before measuring. Spoon lightly into measuring cup. Do not jar cup.

Preheat oven 12 to 20 minutes at required temperature. Leave oven door open first 2 minutes.

Beat whole eggs until thick and piled softly when recipe calls for well-beaten eggs.

Beat egg whites as follows: *Frothy*—entire mass forms bubbles; *Rounded peaks*—peaks turn over slightly when beater is slowly lifted upright; *Stiff peaks*—peaks remain standing when beater is slowly lifted upright.

Beat egg yolks until thick and lemon-colored when recipe calls for well-beaten egg yolks.

Place oven rack so top of product will be almost at center of oven. Stagger pans so no pan is directly over another and they do not touch each other or walls of oven. Place single pan so that center of product is near center of oven.

Covering foods to be stored in the refrigerator will depend upon the type of refrigerator used.

For These Recipes—What To Use

BAKING POWDER—double-action type.

BREAD CRUMBS—one slice fresh bread equals about 1 cup soft crumbs or cubes. One slice dry or toasted bread equals about ¾ cup dry cubes or ⅓ cup fine, dry crumbs.

BUTTERED CRUMBS—soft or dry bread or cracker crumbs tossed in melted butter or margarine.

Use 1 to 2 tablespoons butter or margarine for

1 cup soft crumbs and 2 to 4 tablespoons butter or margarine for 1 cup dry crumbs.

CHOCOLATE—unsweetened chocolate.

CORNSTARCH—thickening agent. One tablespoon has the thickening power of 2 tablespoons flour.

CREAM—light, table or coffee cream, containing not less than 18% butter fat.

HEAVY or WHIPPING CREAM—containing not

less than 36% butter fat.

FLOUR—all-purpose (hard wheat) flour. (In some southern areas where a blend of soft wheat is used, better products may result when minor adjustments are made in recipes. A little less liquid or more flour may be needed.) If cake flour is required, recipe will so state.

GRATED PEEL—whole citrus fruit peel finely grated through colored part only; white is bitter.

OIL—salad, cooking. Use olive oil only when recipe states.

ROTARY BEATER—hand-operated (Dover type) beater or electric mixer.

SHORTENING—a hydrogenated vegetable shortening, all-purpose shortening, butter or margarine. Use lard or oil when specified.

SOUR MILK—sweet milk added to 1 tablespoon vinegar or lemon juice in measuring cup up to 1-cup line and stirred well; or use buttermilk.

SUGAR—granulated (beet or cane).

How To Do It

BASTE—spoon liquid (or use baster) over cooking food to add moisture and flavor.

BLANCH NUTS—the flavor of nuts is best maintained when nuts are allowed to remain in water the shortest possible time during blanching. Therefore, blanch only about ½ cup at a time; repeat as many times as necessary for larger amounts.

Bring to rapid boiling enough water to well cover shelled nuts. Drop in nuts. Turn off heat and allow nuts to remain in the water about 1 min.; drain or remove with fork or slotted spoon. Place between folds of absorbent paper; pat dry. Gently squeeze nuts with fingers to remove skins; or peel. Place on dry absorbent paper. To dry thoroughly, frequently shift nuts to dry spots on paper.

GRATE NUTS—use a rotary-type grater with hand-operating crank. Follow manufacturer's directions. Grated nuts should be fine and light.

GRIND NUTS—put nuts through medium blade of food chopper. Or use electric blender, grinding enough nuts at one time to cover blades. Cover blender container. (Turning motor off and on helps to throw nuts back onto blades.) Grind nuts until particles are still dry enough to remain separate—not oily and compact. Empty container and grind next batch.

TOAST NUTS—place nuts in a shallow baking dish or pie pan and brush lightly with cooking oil. Heat in oven at 350°F until delicately browned. Move and turn nuts occasionally. Or add blanched nuts to a heavy skillet in which butter (about 1 tablespoon per cup of nuts) has been melted; or use oil. Brown lightly over medium heat, constantly turning and moving nuts with a spoon.

SALT NUTS—toast nuts; drain on absorbent paper and sprinkle with salt.

BOIL—cook in liquid in which bubbles rise continually and break on the surface. Boiling temperature of water at sea level is 212°F.

BOILING WATER BATH—set a deep pan on oven rack and place the filled baking dish in pan. Pour boiling water into pan to level of mixture in baking dish. Prevent further boiling by using given oven temperature.

CHILL GELATIN MIXTURES—set dissolved gelatin mixture in refrigerator or in pan of ice and water. If mixture is placed over ice and water, stir frequently; if placed in refrigerator, stir occasionally. Chill gelatin mixtures until slightly thicker than consistency of thick, unbeaten egg white. Then add the remainder of ingredients, such as chopped or whole foods which would sink to the bottom of the mold if the gelatin were not sufficiently thickened. When gelatin mixture is already thick because of ingredients or is not a clear mixture, chill mixture until it begins to gel (gets slightly thicker) before adding chopped or whole foods.

UNMOLD GELATIN—run tip of knife around top edge of mold to loosen. Invert mold onto chilled serving plate. If necessary, wet a clean towel in hot water and wring it almost dry. Wrap hot towel around mold for a few seconds only. If mold does not loosen, repeat.

CRUSH CRUMBS—place cookies, crackers, zwieback or the like on a long length of heavy waxed paper. Loosely fold paper around material to be crushed, tucking under open ends. With a rolling pin, gently crush to make fine crumbs. Or place crackers or cookies in a plastic bag and crush.

If using electric blender, break 5 or 6 crackers, cookies or the like into blender container. Cover container. Blend on low speed, flicking motor on and off until crumbs are medium fine. Empty container and repeat blending until desired amount of crumbs is obtained.

CINNAMON SUGAR—mix thoroughly ¼ cup sugar and 2 teaspoons cinnamon. Use to sugar doughnuts, cookies or toast.

CUT MARSHMALLOWS or DRIED FRUITS (uncooked)—with scissors dipped frequently in water to avoid stickiness.

DICE—cut into small cubes.

FLUTE EDGE of PASTRY—press index finger on edge of pastry, then pinch pastry with thumb and index finger of other hand. Lift fingers and repeat procedure to flute around entire edge.

FOLD—use flexible spatula and slip it down side of bowl to bottom. Turn bowl quarter turn. Lift spatula through mixture along side of bowl with blade parallel to surface. Turn spatula over to fold lifted mixture across material on surface. Cut down and under; turn bowl and repeat process until material seems blended. With every fourth stroke, bring spatula up through center.

GRATE CHOCOLATE—use a rotary-type grater with hand-operating crank. Follow manufacturer's directions. Grated chocolate should be fine and light. Grated chocolate melts more rapidly.

MELT CHOCOLATE—melt over simmering water to avoid scorching.

MEASURE BROWN SUGAR—pack firmly into measuring cup so that sugar will hold shape of cup when turned out.

MINCE—cut or chop into small, fine pieces.

PREPARE DOUBLE-STRENGTH COFFEE BEVERAGE—prepare coffee in usual manner (method and grind of coffee depending upon type of coffee maker), using 4 measuring tablespoons coffee per standard measuring cup water. Use 6 measuring tablespoonsful for **triple-strength coffee.**

SCALD MILK—heat in top of double boiler over simmering water just until a thin film appears.

SIMMER—cook in a liquid just below boiling point; bubbles form slowly and break below surface.

WHIP CREAM—(for use as topping or filling or as an ingredient in a cake) chill bowl, beater and whipping cream. Pour chilled cream into chilled bowl. Using chilled beater, beat (on high speed if using electric mixer) until soft peaks are formed when beater is slowly lifted upright. If whipped cream is to be incorporated into a frozen or refrigerator dessert or salad, beat only until of medium consistency (piles softly).

The maximum amount of cream that should be whipped at one time is 1½ cups. If recipe calls for more than 1½ cups whip 1 cup at a time. Whipping cream doubles in volume when whipped.

OVEN TEMPERATURES—Use a portable oven thermometer for greater accuracy of oven temperatures.

Very slow.................250°F to 275°F
Slow......................300°F to 325°F
Moderate..................350°F to 375°F
Hot.......................400°F to 425°F
Very Hot..................450°F to 475°F
Extremely Hot.............500°F to 525°F

WHEN USING THE ELECTRIC BLENDER—Cover blender container before starting and stopping motor to avoid splashing. To aid even mixing, frequently scrape down sides of container with a rubber spatula, first stopping motor.

To grind, put in blender container enough food at one time to cover blades. Cover; turn on motor and grind until very fine. Turning motor off and on helps to throw food back on blades. Empty container and grind next batch of food.

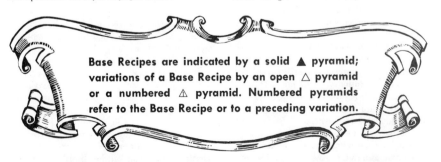

Base Recipes are indicated by a solid ▲ pyramid; variations of a Base Recipe by an open △ pyramid or a numbered ⚠ pyramid. Numbered pyramids refer to the Base Recipe or to a preceding variation.

HOME COOKING in the MICROWAVE OVEN

The microwave oven is truly magical: roasts are done in minutes instead of hours; cookies in less than 3 minutes instead of 20. Almost as magical is the discovery that the microwave oven can produce good home cooking, the kind of cooking which captures the flavors, aromas and textures of an old-fashioned kitchen without the old-fashioned hours spent over a hot stove.

This cookbook tells you the secrets. No more being intimidated by recipes which dictate split-second timing. No more hesitation about whether to try a favorite family recipe in the microwave oven.

TOOLS AND TECHNIQUES—Following are some of the tools and techniques used to assure success and maximum convenience in microwave oven cooking.

Proper Selection Of Pots And Cooking Utensils—Manufacturers' directions will list utensils which can and cannot be used in microwave ovens. For most of our recipes, we used heatproof glassware or paper products, including paper cups and plates. In some cases, we used ingenuity to design our own cookware, for instance, baking sheets made of cardboard. If you don't already own appropriate utensils, the glass dishes are readily available in department or hardware stores and are not expensive.

The single investment we made in special equipment was a microwave-safe "browning skillet," used in many of the recipes for sautéing onions or mushrooms or lightly browning meat. This is a special, microwave-absorbent pan which can be placed empty in the microwave oven (not possible with other kinds of utensils) and preheated. The surface becomes hot and when food is placed on it, is seared or browned as in a conventional skillet. It's available through most microwave oven dealers.

If you do not use a browning skillet, the food will cook in about the same amount of time, but it will not brown and certain nuances of flavor will be lost.

We specify what types of utensils to use.

Covers—Covering cooking containers helps retain heat and moisture and does not retard cooking because microwaves will pass right through them. Some recipes call for covers, some do not. If a cover is not specified in the microwave oven directions, follow the procedure noted in the master recipe.

Use the glass covers which come with the cooking dishes or cover the dish with plastic wrap. It is usually recommended that plastic wrap be punctured in several places to prevent buildup of steam.

Arranging Food In The Oven—The general rule to remember is that food cooks from the outside of the oven in. Where arrangement of food is critical or differs from the general rule, it is specified in the recipes.

Rotating Dishes—To assure even cooking in the oven, it is important to rotate most dishes during the cooking period. Depending on the length of time the food will take to cook, the container should be turned 180 degrees or halfway around at least once, or 90 degrees several times. We specify in each recipe when and how often to rotate.

Stirring—This is one of the secrets of success in microwave cooking and is crucial for such recipes as sauces, gravies, custards and frostings. It blends flavors, prevents curdling of milk and eggs and promotes a uniquely pleasurable texture in the foods which require stirring. Because there is no heat in the microwave oven or the pan, it is much more convenient and safer to stir frequently than it is on the conventional stove. We specify how often to stir with each recipe that requires it. It is important to follow these directions carefully in order to get successful results.

Standing Time—Many dishes cooked in the microwave call for a "standing time" after cooking to allow the flavor and texture to develop to the proper point. This is an essential part of the microwave process and it is important to follow directions. For instance, when meat is finished cooking in the oven, it will often have a somewhat coarse "bloody" taste and grainy texture. This will disappear during the standing time and the flavor and texture will be exactly right when it is time to serve. Leaving it in the oven a longer time will not improve the texture, but will only succeed in overcooking the meat. We tell you exactly what to look for to determine when the food should be taken from the oven and how long to let the dish stand. Usually, the dish must be covered during standing time. Plastic wrap is a satisfactory cover.

OUR TEST CONDITIONS—These recipes were tested with a standard Amana Radarange with three cooking cycles: DEFROST, SLOWCOOK and COOK. We did not use the DEFROST cycle in any recipe. We estimate the SLOWCOOK cycle to be about half the speed of the COOK cycle in our kitchen. We used no special attachments, such as the automatic turntable. All our ingredients were at room temperature and all were purchased at local supermarkets. We used standard cuts of meat and nationally distributed brands of other foods. In other words, we duplicated home conditions. If, because of container or oven size, the amount of food we cooked differs in any way from the master recipe, we specify the adjustment.

We tell you the conditions of our testing because, as any microwave oven user knows, microwave cooking times are easily affected by a number of variables: the type and temperature of the ingredients, the shape and size of individual pieces, the brand of oven and the wattage delivered, and even the size or shape of the container.

HOW TO USE THIS BOOK—First, find the recipe you want to cook. A microwave symbol ![] next to the name of the recipe indicates it is suitable for preparation in the microwave oven. Microwave symbols which are circled indicate a recipe which

produces superlative results. Instructions for preparing the recipe in the microwave oven are given after the master recipe. For some types of foods such as vegetables, instructions, in table form, are located in the introductory material.

Follow the master recipe for amounts of ingredients, instructions on preparing ingredients, sequence of preparation and tests for doneness, noting any deviations from these instructions included in the microwave recipe.

The speed of the cooking cycle (COOK or SLOWCOOK) and approximate cooking times are given in the microwave oven recipe. Also included in the microwave directions are the type and size of utensils, the recommended standing time, if any, and the *OVERALL COOKING TIME*. This figure is the approximate minimum number of minutes it will take to cook the entire recipe and is given in minutes and seconds. For instance, 12 and one-half minutes will be noted as *12:30*. Not included in the *OVERALL COOKING TIME* figure is the time necessary to melt butter or fat since this can vary as much as 2 minutes depending on the temperature of the pan and the type of fat used. Where it is necessary to cook foods in batches, such as when browning meat balls, the *OVERALL COOKING TIME* includes the combined cooking times for all batches. We do not include an *OVERALL COOKING TIME* if one or more of the ingredients, such as a white sauce, must be prepared using a separate recipe.

Since variations exist even for ovens of the same model, it is always best to test the dishes frequently when first using the recipes. The cooking times given in the recipes are minimum recommended cooking times.

Remember that in all microwave oven cooking, the composition of the food being cooked and the total time it is in the oven, as well as the power output, affect the relative cooking time. Foods having low moisture or high fat or sugar contents will cook faster. Also, if the recipe calls for food to be in the oven more than about 10 minutes, the carryover of heat generated by the food itself will contribute to reduce the length of cooking time.

HOME COOKING in the SLOW COOKER

A slow cooker is a small investment in a lot of luxury. In the morning, just plug it in, say a warm goodbye as you go out the door to office or appointments, and come home to a perfectly cooked, ready-to-serve meal with the smells and tastes suggestive of long, loving hours spent in preparation.

We show you which recipes are the best by circling the slow cooker symbol which appears next to the name of appropriate recipes. These dishes adapted most easily and produced outstanding results in the slow cooker.

We have tried to eliminate recipes which call for a combination of cooking in the slow cooker and on the conventional stove. In some recipes, however, we found it necessary to sauté onions or finish sauces on top of the stove. Sautéing onions on top of the stove assures they will finish cooking at the same time as the other ingredients.

We do tell you how to brown or sear meat or other ingredients in the slow cooker. However, browning on the stove does give better color and improve the flavor of some ingredients. We specify in each recipe when this step is necessary; in most cases it is optional. If you do take the option of browning on the stove and it is not specified in the recipe, use the minimum cooking time given. For example, if the range of cooking time is 4 to 6 hours, use 4 hours.

TOOLS AND TECHNIQUES—Following are some of the tools and techniques used to assure success and maximum convenience when cooking with the slow cooker.

Pot Size—We specify the size pot required for each recipe. If a larger pot is substituted for a smaller one, cooking times must be adjusted downward. If the recipe is doubled and the larger pot is used, cooking times remain the same; if the recipe is cut in half and the smaller pot is used, cooking times remain the same.

The Setting—When to use the HIGH and LOW settings are noted with each recipe. If you wish to change the setting from HIGH to LOW (or their equivalent settings on your slow cooker) to extend the cooking time, estimate that it will take about twice as long to cook. If changing the setting from LOW to HIGH, reduce the cooking time by about one-half. In all cases, we provide the guidelines which will help you to judge when the food is fully cooked. You are not dependent on the clock.

Preparing Ingredients—All ingredients were prepared according to the directions given in the master recipe, with a few exceptions noted in individual recipes. Cooking time is affected by the size of the pieces of food. If a recipe calls for meat cut into 1½-in. pieces and you put 3-in. pieces into the pot, the meat will cook more slowly.

HOW TO USE THIS BOOK—First, find the recipe you want to cook. The slow cooker symbol next to the name of the recipe indicates it is suitable for preparation in the slow cooker. Slow cooker symbols which are circled indicate a recipe which produces superlative results. Instructions for preparing the recipe in the slow cooker are given after the master recipe or follow microwave oven instructions, if any. For some types of foods such as cakes, instructions, in table form, are located in the introductory material.

Follow the master recipe for amounts of ingredients, instructions on preparing ingredients, sequence of preparation and tests for doneness, noting deviations given in the slow cooker recipe.

DESSERTS

FRUIT DESSERTS—Fresh fruits in season, with a dash of liqueur, sugar and cream or a topping, if desired, and unelaborated stewed, frozen or canned fruits, are probably the lightest and easiest to prepare of all desserts.

PUDDINGS—Baked, steamed or top-of-the-stove puddings are usually thickened with flour or cornstarch, or with starchy cereals such as tapioca, rice and corn meal. The extent of thickening depends primarily upon the proportion of starch to liquid. Thickening continues as the mixture cools. To make such mixtures smooth, blend until smooth with a little cold liquid after mixing the sugar with the starch; help keep granules separated by constantly stirring while cooking—this also insures uniform heating. Starch mixtures must be brought to boiling and cooked long enough to destroy the starch flavor.

CUSTARDS are mixtures of sweetened and flavored milk and eggs. Thickening is due to the coagulation of the egg proteins on heating.

Baked Custard—The custard mixture thickens in the form of a "gel" in which the coagulated egg protein encloses and holds the liquid. Custards should be baked at a low temperature, because too high a temperature (or too long baking) will cause the protein to toughen and squeeze out liquid. Shorten baking time by scalding the milk before stirring it into the slightly beaten eggs. To insure uniform temperature throughout the mixture, custards are usually baked in a boiling water bath. A baked custard is done when a silver knife inserted halfway between the center and edge of custard comes out clean.

Stirred Custard—The custard mixture is cooked over simmering water with constant stirring until it is just thick enough to coat a silver spoon; it becomes somewhat thicker on cooling. Curdling may occur when the mixture is nearing the proper consistency if the water under the custard is boiling rather than just simmering or is continued too long.

SOUFFLES—This baked product is made light and fluffy by the addition of beaten egg whites. For maximum volume and easy folding into mixture, beat egg whites until they form rounded peaks and do not slide when bowl is partially inverted.

A baked soufflé may be left in the oven for a short time with the heat turned off if it cannot be served immediately. As a soufflé cools it tends to shrink and fall because the volume of air decreases. An underbaked soufflé will fall rapidly; a soufflé baked until done and cooled slowly will fall slowly upon removal from the oven.

TORTES—These are cakelike desserts, made light with eggs and often rich with nuts; white bread crumbs, cracker crumbs or grated nuts sometimes take the place of flour. Tortes differ in texture from cakes, but are handled in much the same way. Cool tortes 15 min. in pans.

REFRIGERATOR DESSERTS must be chilled in refrigerator until firm enough to serve.

FROZEN DESSERTS—Some frozen desserts should be agitated during freezing to break up large ice crystals while they are forming. The smaller the ice crystals in the frozen dessert, the smoother and creamier-seeming will be the texture of the dessert. Therefore, when the dessert is frozen to a mushy consistency it should be removed from the refrigerator and beaten or stirred until smooth. The whipped cream used in mousses prevents formation of large ice crystals by incorporating air into the mixture. Any substance, such as gelatin, eggs, flour, cornstarch and rennet, which increases the viscosity (resistance to pouring) of the mixture tends to separate the crystals and prevent them from growing.

Stirring (agitation) during freezing process— *American ice cream*—mixture of cream, sugar and flavoring. Cream that can be whipped is highly desirable since the incorporation of air during whipping gives a smooth texture to the ice cream. Whipping also distributes the fat evenly, creating added smoothness as the mixture becomes frozen. *French ice cream*—a rich mixture of eggs, cream, sugar and flavorings; virtually a frozen custard. *Philadelphia ice cream*—uncooked mixture of cream, sugar, and flavorings; never with gelatin or other binder added. *Frozen custard*—mixture with a custard base; also a frozen product, in the wholesale and retail trade, too low in butterfat content to be legally called ice cream. *Water ices*—fruit juice which is diluted and sweetened with sugar, sirup or honey; has rather coarse texture, melts easily. *Granites*—water ices frozen with little stirring; rough and icy in texture. *Frappé*—water ice frozen to a mushy consistency. *Sherbet*—water ice (the base of which may be fruit juice, fruit pulp or crushed pulp) with beaten egg white or gelatin added—this decreases the size of crystals and gives a smoother product; milk sherbet uses milk as a part of liquid in the water ice. *Sorbet*—sherbet made of several kinds of fruit. *Coupe*—frozen cup usually composed of fruit and ice cream and attractively garnished with whipped cream, candied fruits and peels, chopped nuts, mint leaves or fresh fruit; originally served in a special glass similar to the "champagne coupe."

Little or no stirring during freezing process—The following are ice creams made of heavy cream with or without eggs: *Parfait*—made by pouring a hot thick sirup over beaten egg whites or beaten egg yolks, adding flavoring and folding in whipped cream. *Biscuit*—parfait or similar mixture, partially frozen, then packed in small individual paper cases and frozen until firm. *Bombe*—two or more frozen mixtures packed in a melon-shaped or round mold and refrozen. *Mousse*—sweetened and flavored whipped cream; may contain gelatin for firmness.

DESSERTS IN THE MICROWAVE OVEN—Desserts such as custards, mousselike puddings and even ice cream are often a challenge to the best of cooks. Cooking in the microwave oven makes many of these recipes virtually failsafe. The texture of the custards and custard bases, puddings and tapiocas are smooth and creamy. Ice cream bases are outstanding and even puddings such as **Holiday Bread Pudding** and **Indian Pudding,** which often dry out in conventional cooking, are moist and delicious cooked in the microwave oven.

Frequent stirring is extremely important to achieve the smooth texture which makes custard-type dishes so good. Each recipe notes when and how often to stir.

Water Baths—Set the covered casserole containing the pudding in a larger dish. Fill the larger dish with boiling water to the level of the pudding. Use a 1½-qt. casserole set in an 8-in. round baking dish or in a 3-qt. casserole.

Steamers—See *Water Baths.* The larger dish is also covered.

Test For Doneness—Begin testing baked and steamed puddings for doneness when they stop bubbling and begin to pull away from the sides of the container. Insert a cake tester between the outside edge and the center of the pudding. When the dish is done, the tester will emerge clean. The custards are done when thick enough to coat a silver spoon.

DESSERTS IN THE SLOW COOKER—The taste of fresh cooked fruits and homemade applesauce are a pleasure which most people enjoy only by remembering Grandmother's kitchen. If you want to revive a little bit of Grandmother's kitchen in your own home, try these cooked fruit recipes in the slow cooker. They are not only as delicious as you remember them, but they are virtually trouble-free to prepare and nutritious. Arrange the ingredients in the slow cooker and forget them, in some as cases for as long as overnight.

The puddings are cooked in the special slow cooker 2-qt. baking tin; you may use a 2-lb. coffee can. Put the pudding mixture in the baking tin, cover the top of the tin securely with plastic wrap and place the tin in the slow cooker. Cover the slow cooker, leaving the top slightly ajar to allow moisture to escape; set the cooker on HIGH for the required number of hours.

The **Holiday Bread Pudding** is cooked without a top on the baking tin, but with paper towels lining the top of the slow cooker (hold them in place with rubber bands) and two or three layers of paper towelling inside the top of the slow cooker. Set the top on the slow cooker, but leave it slightly ajar. For the **New England Pumpkin Pudding,** the top of the baking tin is closed.

Cooking Times—There is not much more than 15 min. leeway on the times we recommend.

Test For Doneness—The puddings are done when they start to pull away from the sides of the tin and when a cake tester inserted in the center comes out clean. Do not open the slow cooker to test the puddings more than 30 min. before the end of the specified cooking time or they will fall.

▲ Stewed Prunes

Set out a medium-size saucepan having a tight-fitting cover.

Rinse thoroughly and put into the saucepan
1 lb. (about 2½ cups) dried prunes
Cover prunes with
1 qt. hot water
Cover pan and allow prunes to soak 1 hr.

Simmer prunes in water in which they have been soaking, 45 to 60 min., or until fruit is plump and tender.

If desired, accompany each serving with a **lemon wedge.** *About 3½ cups Stewed Prunes*

Stewed Prunes

Use a 1½-qt. covered casserole.

Cover and COOK until tender (about 8 min.).

Cover and let stand 5 min.

OVERALL COOKING TIME: 8:00

Stewed Prunes

Use a 3½-qt. slow cooker.

Do not pre-soak prunes.

Put prunes in slow cooker and add water to barely cover.

Cook on LOW for 8 to 10 hrs.

△ Cooked Apricots

Follow ▲ Recipe. Substitute 1 lb. (about 3 cups) **dried apricots** for dried prunes. Cook 40 min., or until fruit is plump and tender.

Cooked Apricots

Follow Recipe with substitution as in △ Recipe.

Creamy Prune Whip

Cooked Apricots

Follow Recipe with changes as in △ Recipe.

Creamy Prune Whip

Put a bowl and a rotary beater into refrigerator to chill.

Prepare
Stewed Prunes (one-half recipe, on this page)
When prunes are tender, drain. Pit the prunes. Force prunes through a sieve or food mill placed over a large bowl.

Stir into the sieved prunes
2 tablespoons lemon juice
Using the chilled bowl and beater, beat until cream is of medium consistency (piles softly)
1 cup chilled whipping cream
Set whipped cream in refrigerator while beating egg whites.

Using clean beater, beat until frothy
2 egg whites
⅛ teaspoon salt
Add gradually, beating well after each addition
½ cup sugar
Beat until rounded peaks are formed.

Spread beaten egg whites and whipped cream over prune mixture and gently fold *(page 7)* together.

Chill thoroughly before serving.

To serve, spoon into sherbet glasses. Top with
Swirls of whipped cream (Sweetened Whipped Cream; *HCL #8*, forced through pastry bag and No. 27 star decorating tube)
Candied Cherries

6 servings

▲ Spiced Applesauce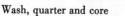

Wash, quarter and core
8 large (about 4 lbs.) cooking apples
Put into large saucepan with
¾ cup water
Cover and simmer 15 to 20 min., or until apples are tender when pierced with a fork. Stir occasionally. Add more water if necessary. Force through a sieve or food mill placed over a saucepan.

Stir in a mixture of
½ cup firmly packed brown sugar
1 teaspoon cinnamon
½ teaspoon nutmeg
and
2 teaspoons lemon juice
Return to low heat and stir until sugar is dissolved.

Serve hot or cold.   *8 to 10 servings*

Spiced Applesauce

Use a 1½-qt. and a 3-qt. casserole.

Put apples and water in large casserole. Cover and COOK until tender (about 10 min.).

Put applesauce mixture in small casserole. COOK uncovered, stirring every 1 min., until sugar is dissolved (about 3 min.).

Cover and let stand 5 min.
OVERALL COOKING TIME: 13:00

Spiced Applesauce

Use a 3½-qt. slow cooker.

Assemble all ingredients in slow cooker, except use only ½ cup water (instead of ¾ cup).

Cook on LOW for 8 to 10 hrs.

△ Fruit Juice Applesauce

Follow ▲ Recipe. Before serving, blend in 2 tablespoons **orange juice** or **pineapple juice.**

Fruit Juice Applesauce

Follow Recipe with addition as in △ Recipe.

Fruit Juice Applesauce

Follow Recipe with changes as in △ Recipe.

▲ Encore Baked Apples

Set out a 2-qt. casserole having a tight-fitting cover.

Select and wash
6 medium-size (about 2 lbs.) firm cooking apples
Core by inserting corer in stem end and cutting toward blossom end. Push halfway into apple. Remove corer and insert in opposite end. Make a complete turn with corer in both ends. Remove all the core. Pare upper fourth of each apple. Arrange apples in casserole, pared sides up.

Mix together
¾ cup firmly packed brown sugar
2 teaspoons cinnamon
Fill cavity of each apple with about 2 tablespoons cinnamon-sugar mixture. Allowing ½ teaspoon for each apple, dot tops with
1 tablespoon butter or margarine
Pour into casserole
Water, to a depth of ½ in.
(unsweetened fruit juice may be used as part of liquid)

Cover and bake at 350°F 45 to 50 min., or until apples are tender when gently pierced with a fork. Or bake uncovered and baste frequently with liquid from bottom of casserole.

6 servings

Encore Baked Apples

Use an 11-in. oblong baking dish.

COOK uncovered, rotating pan every 5 min., until apples are tender (about 15 min.).

Cover and let stand 5 min.

OVERALL COOKING TIME: 15:00

Encore Baked Apples

Use a 5-qt. slow cooker.

Arrange apples in slow cooker. Add water to a depth of ¼ in. (instead of ½ in.), just to keep apples from sticking to the bottom of the slow cooker.

Cook on LOW for 5 to 6 hrs.

▲ Variety Baked Apples

Follow ▲ Recipe for coring and paring apples. In center cavity of each apple, place one of the following mixtures: 2 tablespoons **mincemeat** mixed with 1 teaspoon **orange juice;** 1 tablespoon finely chopped **nuts** mixed with 1 tablespoon **granulated** or **brown sugar;** 2 tablespoons mixed chopped **nuts, raisins,** chopped **dates** or **figs;** or 2 tablespoons thick **cranberry sauce** or **jelly.** Dot with butter or margarine as in ▲ Recipe.

Variety Baked Apples

Follow Recipe with changes as in ⚠ Recipe.

Baked Apples with Meringue

Variety Baked Apples

Follow Recipe with changes as in ⚠ Recipe.

⚠ Baked Apples with Meringue

Follow ▲ Recipe; instead of water, use a sirup made by boiling ¾ cup **sugar** and 1 cup **water** for 5 min. Bake apples uncovered 30 to 40 min., or until almost tender, basting frequently with sirup. Remove from oven and cool in sirup. Pile meringue on apples. Bake at 350°F 10 to 15 min., or until meringue is delicately browned.

For Meringue—Beat 2 **egg whites** until frothy; gradually beat in ¼ cup **sugar;** beat until rounded peaks are formed and egg whites do not slide when bowl is partially inverted.

Cherries Jubilee

Set out a chafing dish or saucepan. Chill desired number of serving dishes in refrigerator.

Set aside to drain thoroughly, reserving sirup, contents of

**1 No. 2 can pitted Bing cherries
(about 2½ cups, drained)**

Put the reserved cherry sirup into the chafing dish or saucepan.

Stirring occasionally, bring sirup to boiling over direct heat. Boil about 10 min., or until slightly thicker. Mix in the drained cherries and heat in chafing dish over pan of simmering water (or low heat) until cherries are thoroughly heated. With spoon, gently move cherries in pan occasionally.

When ready to serve, spoon into the chilled serving dishes
> **1 qt. vanilla ice cream**

Heat thoroughly in a small saucepan
> **⅔ cup brandy**

Ignite with match until brandy flames and pour over the cherries. Immediately spoon flaming cherries over ice cream and serve while still flaming. *6 to 8 servings*

Cherries Jubilee

Use a 1½-qt. casserole.

COOK cherry sirup, stirring every 1 min., until boiling and slightly thickened (about 5 min.).

Mix in cherries and COOK, stirring every 2 min., until heated (about 5 min.).
OVERALL COOKING TIME: 10:00

Bananas Guadalcanal
MR. P. PLOWMAN, PAGO PAGO,
TUTUILA, AMERICAN SAMOA

Lightly butter an 8x8x2-in. baking dish.

Mix together and set aside
> **2 tablespoons water**
> **1 teaspoon vanilla extract**
> **½ teaspoon orange extract**
> **½ teaspoon almond extract**

(Two tablespoons rum, claret, cherry brandy or liqueur may be substituted for the above.)

Peel
> **4 bananas with all-yellow or**
> **green-tipped peel**

Measure onto waxed paper
> **5 tablespoons brown sugar**

Roll bananas in brown sugar and place one-half inch apart in baking dish. Sprinkle with the flavoring mixture, rum, or liqueur.

Bake at 350°F 25 min., or until bananas are completely tender. During baking, baste the bananas two or three times with the sirup that has formed.

Serve hot with **cream** or cooled with **Favorite Vanilla Ice Cream** *(page 42)* topped with remaining sirup. *4 servings*

▲ Banana Fritters

A deep saucepan or automatic deep-fryer for deep-frying will be needed.

Peel, cut into 1½-in. crosswise pieces and put into a bowl
> **4 firm bananas with all-yellow peel**

Gently toss banana pieces with a mixture of
> **3 tablespoons confectioners' sugar**
> **2 tablespoons lemon juice**
> **1½ tablespoons rum or kirsch**

Cover bowl and allow banana pieces to marinate 45 min. to 1 hr., turning occasionally.

Fill deep saucepan with fat and heat to 365°F

Sift together into a bowl and set aside
> **1⅓ cups sifted flour**
> **2 tablespoons sugar**
> **1 teaspoon baking powder**
> **½ teaspoon salt**

Melt and set aside to cool
> **1 tablespoon shortening**

Drain banana pieces and set aside, reserving liquid for fritter batter.

Beat until thick and lemon-colored
> **2 egg yolks**

Beat in until blended, the melted shortening, the reserved liquid from bananas and
> **⅔ cup milk**
> **1 teaspoon vanilla extract**

Make a well in center of dry ingredients. Pour

in liquid mixture all at one time and blend just until batter is smooth.

Beat until rounded peaks are formed
  2 egg whites
Spread beaten egg whites over batter and gently fold *(page 7)* together.

Coat banana pieces by rolling in shallow pan containing
  ¼ cup flour
Using a large fork or slotted spoon, dip banana pieces into batter and coat evenly. Drain excess batter from banana pieces before deep-frying. Deep-fry only as many fritters at one time as will float uncrowded one layer deep in the heated fat. Turn fritters with tongs or a fork as they rise to surface of fat and frequently thereafter (do not pierce). Deep-fry 2 to 3 min., or until golden brown.

Drain fritters over fat for a few seconds before removing to absorbent paper.

Sift over fritters
  Vanilla Confectioners' Sugar
  (HCL #8)
Serve immediately.   *About 6 servings*

△ **Strawberry Fritters**

Follow ▲ Recipe; substitute for bananas 1 qt. large firm **strawberries,** rinsed and hulled. Do not marinate strawberries. Add the rum to the batter; omit lemon juice. Increase the confectioners' sugar to ½ cup and roll the strawberries in it (instead of in flour) before dipping into the batter. Increase flour in batter to 1½ cups.

Blushing Pears

Set out a shallow baking dish having a cover.

Wash, cut into halves, core and pare
  2 large or 4 small pears
Cut three tiny slits in full part of each rounded side. Insert in each slit
  Red cinnamon candy

Place pears in baking dish, cut side down. Pour into dish
  ¼ cup water
  2 tablespoons lemon juice
Cover and bake at 350°F 30 to 50 min. (depending upon size and variety of pears), or until pears are tender when gently pierced with a fork.

Remove pears from oven. Turn pears and fill the center of each half with (in order)
  1 tablespoon brown or granulated
  sugar
  ½ teaspoon grated lemon peel   *(page 6)*
  ¼ teaspoon butter or margarine
  Sprinkling of cinnamon or nutmeg
Return baking dish to oven uncovered and leave until pears are glazed.

Serve hot or chilled.   *4 servings*

Note: For variety, substitute for sugar, butter and spices in each pear center 2 teaspoons colorful tart **jelly** such as currant, mint or cranberry, or orange marmalade.

Blushing Pears

Use a baking dish.

COOK pears in water and lemon juice, rotating pan every 5 min., until tender (about 15 min.).

COOK filled pears uncovered until sugar melts to form glaze (about 5 min.).

Cover and let stand 5 min.
          OVERALL COOKING TIME: 20:00

Blushing Pears

Use a 3½-qt. slow cooker.

Place all ingredients, including sugar mixture, in slow cooker.

Cover and cook on LOW for 5 to 6 hours.

Stewed Rhubarb

Serve refreshingly cold or pleasantly warm.

Set out a 2-qt. saucepan having a tight-fitting cover.

Wash, cut off leaves and ends of stems and cut into 1-in. pieces enough rhubarb to yield
    4 cups (about 1 lb.) fresh rhubarb
(Peel stalks only if skin is tough.)

Put the rhubarb into the saucepan.

Mix together and add to rhubarb
    ¾ cup sugar
    1 teaspoon grated lemon peel *(page 7)*
    ½ teaspoon cinnamon
Drizzle with
    2 teaspoons lemon juice
Put over low heat. Stir until sugar dissolves and a sirup is formed. Cover and cook slowly about 15 min., or until rhubarb is tender.

If deeper pink is desired, carefully stir in
    Few drops red food coloring
Serve hot or cold.   *4 or 5 servings*

Note: If your yen for rhubarb happens to fall on "baking day," this recipe may also be prepared in a casserole-in the oven. Prepare the rhubarb the same way, but put it into a casserole instead, cover and bake at 325°F about 25 min., or until rhubarb is tender when pierced with a fork.

Strawberries with Cream Cheese

VIRGINIA H. AUDAS, CANASTOTA, N. Y.

Sort, rinse, drain and hull
    4 cups (1 qt.) fresh, ripe strawberries
Sweeten strawberries with
    ½ cup sifted confectioners' sugar
Spoon into serving dishes.

Put into a small bowl and beat until light and fluffy
    3 oz. (1 pkg.) cream cheese, softened
    ¼ teaspoon salt

Add gradually and beat until well blended
    ⅓ cup milk or cream
Pour over individual servings.   *4 servings*

Note: Two 1-lb. packages **frozen strawberries** may be substituted for the quart of fresh strawberries; omit sugar.

Flan De Piña
(Pineapple Custard)
LUCILE M. BOGUE
STEAMBOAT SPRINGS, COLO.

Set out a 1½-qt. casserole. Heat water for boiling water bath *(page 6)*.

For Custard—Mix together in a saucepan
    2 cups unsweetened pineapple juice
    2 cups sugar
Stir over medium heat until sugar is dissolved. Remove from heat.

Beat slightly
    4 eggs
    1 egg yolk
    ⅛ teaspoon salt
Stirring constantly, gradually add pineapple mixture to egg mixture. Strain into casserole.

Bake in boiling water bath at 325°F 1½ hrs.

Set aside to cool until lukewarm and immediately chill in refrigerator.

Meanwhile, prepare Caramel Sauce.

For Caramel Sauce—Melt in a heavy light-colored skillet (a black skillet makes it difficult to see the color of the sirup) over low heat
    1 cup sugar
With back of wooden spoon, gently keep sugar moving toward center of skillet until sugar is completely melted and of a golden brown color (lighter than for burnt sugar sirup).

Remove from heat and gradually add, a very small amount at a time
    ½ cup boiling water
(Be careful that steam does not burn hand.) Return to low heat and continue to stir until bubbles are size of dimes. Set aside.

Sift together into a saucepan
1 cup sugar
¼ cup sifted flour
Add gradually, stirring constantly
2 cups boiling water
Continue to stir; bring to boiling and simmer sauce 5 min.

Remove from heat and blend in
2 tablespoons butter
Return to low heat. Stirring constantly, blend in the caramel sirup. Cool slightly and serve over Flan De Piña. *6 to 8 servings*

Caramel-Glazed Custard

▲ Baked Custard

Heat water for boiling water bath *(page 6)*. Set out 4 heat-resistant custard cups.

Scald *(page 7)* in top of double boiler
2 cups milk
Beat slightly
3 eggs
Add and beat just until blended
¼ cup sugar
⅛ teaspoon salt
Stirring constantly, gradually add scalded milk to egg mixture. Strain mixture.

Blend in
2 teaspoons vanilla extract
Pour immediately into custard cups and sprinkle each serving with
Nutmeg
Bake in boiling water bath at 325°F 30 to 45 min., or until a silver knife comes out clean when inserted halfway between center and edge of custard.

Serve warm or chilled. *4 servings*

△ Caramel-Glazed Custard

Set out 5 heat-resistant custard cups.

To Prepare Caramel Glaze—Put ¼ cup **sugar** in a small light-colored heavy skillet. Stir over low heat until sugar is melted and becomes a golden brown sirup. Remove from heat and quickly drizzle on bottom and sides of each custard cup. For a thin, even glaze, twirl custard cup while pouring. Set aside while preparing custard.

Follow ▲ Recipe. Pour custard over sirup in custard cups. Bake in boiling water bath at 325°F 30 to 35 min., or until custard tests done. Remove carefully from boiling water bath. Set on a cooling rack until lukewarm. Chill thoroughly in refrigerator.

When ready to serve, unmold by running a knife around inside edge of custard cups; invert onto chilled serving dishes. The top will be caramel coated and the excess coating will run down the sides to form a sauce at the base of the custard mixture.

Lemon Cake-Top Pudding

MRS. VERNON SHEAN, ROCK ISLAND, ILL.

Grease a 2-qt. casserole. Heat water for boiling water bath *(page 6)*.

Melt and set aside to cool
2 tablespoons butter
Sift into a large bowl
1 cup sugar
½ cup sifted flour
½ teaspoon baking powder
¼ teaspoon salt

Beat until thick and lemon-colored
3 egg yolks
¼ cup lemon juice
2 teaspoons grated lemon peel
(page 6)
Stir into the egg-yolk mixture the melted butter and
1½ cups milk
Stir mixture into dry ingredients.

Beat until frothy
3 egg whites
Add gradually, beating well after each addition
½ cup sugar
Spread beaten egg whites over batter and gently fold *(page 7)* together. Turn batter into casserole.

Bake in boiling water bath at 350°F 50 min., or until a cake tester or wooden pick inserted in center of casserole comes out clean.

6 to 8 servings

Lemon Cake-Top Pudding

Use a 1½-qt. casserole.

Prepare boiling water bath . *(page 12)*

COOK to melt butter (about 1½ min.).

Pour pudding in small casserole, set into water bath. COOK uncovered until tester comes out clean (about 20 min.).
OVERALL COOKING TIME: 21:30

▲ Indian Pudding

Butter a 1½-qt. casserole.

Scald *(page 7)* in top of double boiler
3 cups milk
Remove from heat. Stirring constantly gradually add milk to a mixture of
½ cup yellow corn meal
¼ cup sugar
1 teaspoon salt
1 teaspoon cinnamon
½ teaspoon ginger

Wash double-boiler top to remove scum.

Vigorously stir about 3 tablespoons hot mixture into a mixture of
1 egg, well beaten
½ cup molasses
Immediately blend the molasses mixture into the corn meal mixture. Cook over simmering water about 20 min., or until very thick, stirring constantly. Blend in
2 tablespoons butter or margarine
Turn into casserole. Carefully pour over top
1 cup cold milk
Bake at 300°F 2½ to 3 hrs., or until a silver knife comes out clear when inserted halfway between center and edge of casserole.

Serve warm with **Vanilla Hard Sauce** *(HCL #4)* or **Sweetened Whipped Cream** *(HCL #8)* or **vanilla ice cream.** *About 6 servings*

Indian Pudding

Use a small casserole for the milk and a 1½-qt. casserole. *Do not butter.*

COOK to scald 3 cups milk (about 3 min.).

Stir cornmeal mixture into milk with a wire whisk. Add egg-molasses mixture and COOK uncovered, stirring every 30 sec., until very thick (about 5 min.). Blend in butter and transfer to larger casserole.

Add remaining milk and COOK, rotating pan every 2 min., until knife comes out clean (about 30 min.).
OVERALL COOKING TIME: 43:00

△ Date-Nut Indian Pudding

Follow ▲ Recipe. Blend in with the butter ½ cup chopped **nuts** and ¼ cup cut **dates**.

Date-Nut Indian Pudding

Follow Recipe with additions as in △ Recipe.

Holiday Bread Pudding

Butter a shallow 2-qt. casserole.

Scald *(page 7)*
   3 cups milk
Meanwhile, toast until very crisp and cut into
½-in. cubes
   **5 to 6 slices bread (about 4 cups
      toast cubes)**
Put cubes into the casserole. Drizzle over
cubes while turning them lightly with a fork
   **3 tablespoons melted butter or
      margarine**
Add and mix thoroughly with fork
   **½ cup (3 oz.) mixed candied fruits
   ½ cup (about 3 oz.) golden raisins
   ½ cup (about 2 oz.) coarsely
      chopped black walnuts
   8 to 10 maraschino cherries, quartered
      and well drained**
Set aside.

Blend together
   **3 eggs, slightly beaten
   ½ cup sugar
   ½ teaspoon nutmeg
   ½ teaspoon cinnamon
   ½ teaspoon allspice**
Add the scalded milk gradually, stirring constantly. Pour over bread cube mixture; turn
with fork to blend well.

Bake at 325°F 35 to 45 min., or until a silver
knife comes out clean when inserted halfway
between center and edge of casserole.

Date-Nut Indian Pudding

Meanwhile, prepare
   **Creamy Orange Custard Sauce
   (HCL #4;   substitute 2 whole eggs
      for the 4 egg yolks)**
Serve pudding warm with warm custard sauce
and sprinkle with
   Nutmeg
Serve immediately.   *7 to 8 servings*

Holiday Bread Pudding

Use a 2-qt. casserole for the pudding, a small
casserole for the milk and a baking dish for the
bread crumbs. *Do not butter.*

COOK to scald milk (about 3 min.). COOK to
crisp bread, tossing every 2 min. (about 5 min.).

COOK assembled pudding covered, rotating pan
every 2 min., until a knife comes out clean
(about 15 min.).

OVERALL COOKING TIME: 28:00

Holiday Bread Pudding

Use a 3½-qt. slow cooker with a 2-qt. baking tin.

Line bottom of baking tin with ungreased
waxed paper.

Fill baking tin with pudding mixture. Do not
cover. Lay paper towels on top of slow cooker.
Also line the lid of the slow cooker with paper
towelling held in place with rubber bands.
Leave cover of slow cooker slightly ajar.

Cook on HIGH for 3 to 3½ hrs.

Mocha Fudge Pudding
MRS. WARREN PURCELL, PETERSBURG, VA.

Grease a 1½-qt. casserole.

Mix together thoroughly and set aside
   **¾ cup firmly packed brown sugar
   ¼ cup cocoa**
Melt and set aside to cool
   2 tablespoons butter or margarine

Coarsely chop and set aside
¾ cup (about 3 oz.) walnuts
Sift together into a large bowl
1 cup sifted cake flour
¾ cup sugar
2 tablespoons cocoa
2 teaspoons baking powder
¼ teaspoon salt
Combine
½ cup milk
1 teaspoon vanilla extract
Add the melted butter or margarine and the milk mixture all at one time to dry ingredients. Stir until thoroughly blended. Blend in the chopped nuts.

Turn batter into the casserole. Sprinkle over batter the brown-sugar-cocoa mixture.

Pour over top of batter
1¼ cups hot double-strength coffee beverage *(page 7)*
Bake at 350°F 40 to 45 min.

Serve warm with **heavy cream, whipped cream** or **vanilla ice cream.**   *6 to 8 servings*

Mocha Fudge Pudding

Use a 1½-qt. casserole for the pudding and a small dish to melt butter. *Do not grease.*

COOK to melt butter.

COOK assembled pudding, rotating pan every 1 min., until a knife comes out clean.
                    OVERALL COOKING TIME: 18:00

New England Pumpkin Pudding

One of America's favorites—fragrant, spicy pumpkin pudding.

Butter a 1½-qt. casserole.

Mix together
2 cups (1 1-lb. can) canned pumpkin

New England Pumpkin Pudding

and a mixture of
¾ cup firmly packed brown sugar
1 teaspoon cinnamon
¾ teaspoon salt
½ teaspoon nutmeg
½ teaspoon ginger
¼ teaspoon cloves
Blend together and add, mixing until smooth
3 eggs, slightly beaten
1 cup heavy cream
¾ cup milk
Pour pumpkin mixture into the casserole.

Bake at 350°F about 1 hr., or until a silver knife comes out clean when inserted halfway between center and edge of casserole.

Cool slightly. Decorate, if desired, with
Sweetened Whipped Cream (one-half recipe, HCL #8) or Vanilla Hard Sauce (HCL #4)
Force through a pastry bag and a No. 27 star tube to form a lattice design on top of pudding.
                    6 to 8 servings

New England Pumpkin Pudding

Use a 1½-qt. casserole. *Do not grease.*

COOK assembled pudding, rotating pan every 2 min., until a knife comes out clean (about 20 min.).

                    OVERALL COOKING TIME: 20:00

New England Pumpkin Pudding

Use a 3½-qt. slow cooker with a 2-qt. baking tin.

Line bottom of baking tin with waxed paper. *Do not grease.* Fill tin with pudding mixture and cover. Lay paper towelling on top of slow cooker; also line lid of slow cooker with paper towels held in place with rubber bands. Leave slow cooker lid slightly ajar.

Cook on HIGH for 4 to 4½ hrs.

▲ Soft Custard

Scald *(page 7)* in top of double boiler
 2 cups milk
Beat slightly
 3 eggs
Add and beat just until blended
 ¼ cup sugar
 ⅛ teaspoon salt
Stirring constantly, gradually add scalded milk to the egg mixture.

Wash double-boiler top to remove scum.

Strain mixture into double-boiler top and place over simmering water, stirring constantly and rapidly until mixture coats a silver spoon.

Remove from simmering water at once. Cool to lukewarm over cold water. Blend in
 2 teaspoons vanilla extract
Pour into 4 sherbet glasses and immediately chill in refrigerator.

Coarsely chop
 ¼ cup (about 1 oz.) nuts
Sprinkle 1 tablespoon of the nuts over each serving. *4 servings*

Soft Custard

Use a small casserole.

COOK to scald milk (about 5 min.). Blend in eggs, sugar and salt. Strain into a clean casserole.

COOK, stirring every 1 min., until slightly thickened and will coat a silver spoon (about 5 min.).

OVERALL COOKING TIME: 10:00

△ Fruit Custard

Follow ▲ Recipe. Pour custard over **orange sections** or well-drained **fruit.**

Fruit Custard

Follow **1** Recipe with addition as in △ Recipe.

△ Minty Custard

Follow ▲ Recipe. Prepare **Sweetened Whipped Cream** (one-half recipe, *HCL #8*). Add 1 or 2 drops **peppermint extract** with vanilla extract. Alternate layers of custard and whipped cream in sherbet glasses, ending with whipped cream.

Minty Custard **3**

Follow **1** Recipe with changes as in △ Recipe.

△ Floating Island

Double ▲ Recipe. Beat 2 **egg whites** until frothy. Add ⅛ teaspoon **salt** and ¼ teaspoon **vanilla extract.** Add gradually ¼ cup **sugar,** beating well after each addition and continuing to beat until rounded peaks are formed. Drop by tablespoonfuls into 2 cups scalding **milk** *(page 7).* Do not cover. Cook over simmering water about 5 min., or until set. Remove meringues with a slotted spoon and drain on absorbent paper. Float on chilled soft custard. If desired, top each meringue with a **strawberry** and accompany with additional strawberries.

▲ Tapioca Cream

Set out a 1-qt. saucepan.

Beat until frothy
2 egg whites
Add gradually, beating well after each addition
¼ cup sugar
Beat until rounded peaks are formed.

Put into the saucepan
2 egg yolks, slightly beaten
Add gradually, stirring in
3 cups milk
Add, stirring well
⅓ cup quick-cooking tapioca
¼ to ⅓ cup sugar
¼ teaspoon salt
Set over medium heat and bring mixture to a full boil (about 5 to 8 min.), stirring constantly. Do not overcook.

Remove from heat and stir a small amount of hot tapioca mixture gradually into egg whites. Then quickly blend in remaining tapioca mixture. Blend in
1½ teaspoons vanilla extract
Cool, stirring once after 15 to 20 min. Spoon into serving dishes.   *8 servings*

Tapioca Cream

Use a 1½-qt. casserole.

COOK tapioca mixture, stirring every 30 sec., until boiling (about 5 min.).
OVERALL COOKING TIME: 5:00

△ Peach Tapioca Cream

Follow ▲ Recipe. Arrange **sliced peaches** in serving dishes. Top with chilled tapioca cream.

Peach Tapioca Cream

Follow Recipe with additions as in △ Recipe.

△ Chocolate Tapioca Cream

Follow ▲ Recipe. Add 2 sq. (2 oz.) **chocolate,** cut in pieces, after milk addition.

Chocolate Tapioca Cream

Follow Recipe with addition as in △ Recipe.

△ Peppermint Tapioca Cream

Follow ▲ Recipe. Add ½ cup crushed **peppermint-stick candy** with the vanilla extract.

Peppermint Tapioca Cream

Follow Recipe with addition as in △ Recipe.

Lemon Soufflé
MRS. DALE RILEY, CLARKSBURG, W. VA.

Butter bottom of a 2-qt. casserole. Heat water for boiling water bath *(page 6)*.

Mix thoroughly in a saucepan
½ cup sugar
4½ teaspoons cornstarch
Add gradually, stirring in
1½ cups milk
Set over direct heat and bring rapidly to boiling, stirring constantly; cook 3 min. longer. Cool slightly.

Beat until thick and lemon-colored
3 egg yolks
2 tablespoons plus 1 teaspoon lemon juice
1 tablespoon grated lemon peel (page 6)
Stirring vigorously to blend, pour sauce slowly into egg-yolk mixture. Cool to lukewarm.

Beat until frothy
3 egg whites

Add gradually, beating well after each addition
¼ cup sugar
Beat until rounded peaks are formed.

Spread egg-yolk mixture over beaten egg whites and carefully fold *(page 7)* together.

Bake in boiling water bath at 350°F 1 hr. or until a silver knife, inserted halfway between center and edge, comes out clean.

Serve immediately. *8 servings*

Chocolate Soufflé

MRS. JAMES C. FAHL, WASHINGTON, D. C.

Butter bottom of a 1½-qt. casserole. Heat water for boiling water bath *(page 6)*.

Heat in top of double boiler over simmering water until chocolate is melted and milk is scalded *(page 7)*
½ cup milk
2 sq. (2 oz.) chocolate

Blend with rotary beater and set aside.

Mix together
⅓ cup sugar
3 tablespoons flour
Add gradually, stirring in
½ cup cold milk
2 tablespoons water
Add to mixture in double boiler. Cook over simmering water until thickened, stirring constantly. Continue cooking 5 to 7 min., stirring occasionally.

Meanwhile, beat until thick and lemon-colored
4 egg yolks
Remove about 3 tablespoons chocolate mixture and stir vigorously into beaten egg yolks. Immediately blend into mixture in double boiler and cook 3 to 5 min., stirring constantly. Remove from heat and blend in
2 tablespoons butter or margarine
1 teaspoon vanilla extract
Set aside.

Beat until rounded peaks are formed
4 egg whites

Chocolate Soufflé

Fold *(page 7)* chocolate mixture quickly into beaten egg whites. Turn into casserole.

Bake in boiling water bath at 325°F 1 hr. and 10 min., or until a silver knife, inserted halfway between center and edge, comes out clean.

Serve immediately. *6 servings*

Casserole Cottage-Cheese Cake

A delicate concoction that can be served warm.

Butter a shallow 1½-qt. casserole.

Crush *(page 6)*
12 vanilla wafers (or enough to yield ½ cup crumbs)
Turn crumbs into a bowl. Add gradually, stirring in with a fork
3 tablespoons butter or margarine, melted
With back of spoon, press crumb mixture very firmly in an even layer on bottom of casserole.

Bake at 325°F 5 min. Remove from oven and set aside to cool.

Sift together and set aside
⅓ cup sugar
3 tablespoons flour
¼ teaspoon salt

Force through a sieve or a food mill into a bowl and set aside

1½ cups cream-style cottage cheese

Beat until thick and lemon-colored

4 egg yolks

Combine egg yolks with the cottage cheese and

½ cup cream or undiluted evaporated milk
1 teaspoon lemon juice
½ teaspoon grated lemon peel *(page 6)*
½ teaspoon vanilla extract

Blend thoroughly. Stir in the dry ingredients.

Beat until rounded peaks are formed

4 egg whites

Spread beaten egg whites over cheese mixture and gently fold *(page 7)* together.

Turn into the casserole and sprinkle with

Nutmeg

Bake at 325°F 1 to 1½ hrs., or until a silver knife inserted halfway between center and edge of casserole comes out clean.

Serve warm. If desired, serve with **Sweetened Whipped Cream** *(HCL #8).*   *4 to 6 servings*

Luscious Lemon Cheese Cake

Butter the bottom and sides of a 9-in. spring-form pan.

For Crust—Crush *(page 6)*
24 slices (6 oz.) zwieback (or enough to yield 2⅔ cups crumbs)
Turn crumbs into a bowl. Stir in
½ cup sifted confectioners' sugar
1½ teaspoons grated lemon peel (page 6)
Using a fork, evenly blend with
½ cup butter or margarine, softened
Turn into spring-form pan, reserving ¾ cup for topping. Using fingers or back of spoon, press crumbs very firmly into an even layer on bottom and sides of pan to rim; set aside.

For Filling—Combine and beat until smooth and fluffy

2½ lbs. cream cheese, softened
1¾ cups sugar (add gradually)
3 tablespoons flour
1½ teaspoons grated lemon peel
½ teaspoon vanilla extract

Add in thirds, beating well after each addition, a mixture of

5 eggs, slightly beaten
2 egg yolks

Blend in

¼ cup heavy cream

Turn into pan. Spread evenly. Sprinkle reserved crumb mixture over top.

Bake at 250°F 1 hr. Turn off heat. Let stand in oven 1 hr. longer. Remove to cooling rack to cool completely (4 to 6 hrs.).

Chill in refrigerator several hours or overnight.   *16 to 20 servings*

Luscious Lemon Cheese Cake

Use an 8-in. round baking pan. *Do not grease.*

Assemble cake and SLOWCOOK uncovered, rotating pan every 2 min., until filling is set (about 20 min.).

Let stand until cool.

OVERALL COOKING TIME: 20:00

Old-Fashioned English Plum Pudding

MRS. R. M. HERKENRATT
NORTHFIELD, MINN.

Grease a 2-qt. mold or two 1-qt. molds.

Coarsely chop
1 cup (about 4 oz.) walnuts
¾ cup (about 4 oz.) blanched almonds (page 6)
Mix the chopped nuts with
½ lb. (about 1¼ cups) diced, assorted candied fruits
2 cups (about 10 oz.) seedless raisins
2 cups fine, dry bread crumbs (page 5)
Set aside.

Break apart, discarding membrane which coats it, finely chop and set aside

6 oz. suet (about 1½ cups, chopped)

Sift together in a large bowl

2 cups plus 2 tablespoons sifted flour
2 tablespoons sugar
½ teaspoon baking soda
½ teaspoon salt
1½ teaspoons cinnamon
1¼ teaspoons nutmeg
¾ teaspoon cloves
Few grains allspice

Blend in

½ cup plus 2 tablespoons firmly packed brown sugar

Blend the fruit-nut mixture and the suet into the dry ingredients. Set aside.

Blend together thoroughly

4 eggs, slightly beaten
½ cup molasses
½ cup milk
¼ cup double-strength coffee beverage
(page 7)

Add liquid ingredients to dry ingredients, mixing until well blended. Turn batter into mold, filling about two-thirds full.

Cover mold tightly with greased lid or tie on aluminum foil, parchment paper or 2 layers of waxed paper. Place on trivet or rack in steamer or deep kettle with tight-fitting cover. Pour boiling water into bottom of steamer (enough to continue boiling throughout entire steaming period, if possible). If necessary, quickly add more boiling water during cooking period. Tightly cover steamer and steam 3 hrs. Keep water boiling at all times.

Remove pudding from steamer and immediately loosen edges of pudding with spatula. Unmold onto serving plate.

Serve with

Vanilla Hard Sauce (HCL #4)

About 16 servings

Note: If pudding is to be stored several days, unmold onto cooling rack. Let stand until cold. Wrap in aluminum foil or moisture-vapor-proof material and store in cool place. Steam thoroughly before serving (1 to 2 hrs.).

To Flame a Plum Pudding—Heat **brandy** in a small saucepan. Ignite brandy with match and pour over top of pudding. Serve when flaming stops.

Old-Fashioned English Plum Pudding

Use a 1½-qt. casserole and a 3-qt. casserole as the steamer (see preceding introduction).

Put casserole in steamer, cover and COOK, rotating every 2 min., until bubbling stops and pudding starts to pull away from the pan sides. Test with cake tester; it should come out clean.

OVERALL COOKING TIME: 60:00

Steamed Chocolate Pudding

Grease a 1½-qt. mold.

Melt *(page 7)* and set aside to cool

3 sq. (3 oz.) chocolate

Sift together and set aside

1½ cups sifted flour
1½ teaspoons baking powder
½ teaspoon salt

Cream together until shortening is softened

⅔ cup shortening
1½ teaspoons vanilla extract

Add gradually, creaming until fluffy after each addition

¾ cup sugar

Add in thirds, beating well after each addition

2 eggs, well beaten

Blend in chocolate.

Measure

¾ cup milk

Beating only until blended after each addition, alternately add dry ingredients in fourths, milk in thirds, to creamed mixture. Finally beat only until blended (do not overbeat). Turn batter into mold.

Cover mold tightly with greased lid or tie on aluminum foil, parchment paper or 2 layers of waxed paper. Place on trivet or rack in steamer or deep kettle with tight-fitting cover. Pour boiling water into bottom of steamer (enough to continue boiling throughout entire steaming period if possible). If necessary, quickly add more boiling water during cooking period. Tightly cover steamer and steam 1½ hrs. Keep water boiling at all times.

Remove pudding from steamer and immediately loosen edges of pudding with a spatula. Unmold onto serving plate.

If desired, garnish pudding with
>   ¼ cup (about 1½ oz.) seedless raisins
>   4 pecan halves
>   4 candied cherries
Serve hot with **Sweetened Whipped Cream**

6 to 8 servings

Steamed Chocolate Pudding

Use a 1½-qt. casserole. *Do not grease.* Use a 3-qt. casserole as the steamer (see preceding introduction).

COOK to melt chocolate (about 3 min.).

Put pudding in casserole and place in steamer. Cover with a greased lid. COOK, rotating every 2 min., until bubbling stops and it starts to pull away from the pan sides (about 10 min.). Then test with a knife or cake tester; it should come out clean.

OVERALL COOKING TIME: 13:00

Steamed Chocolate Pudding

Use a 5-qt. slow cooker and a 1-qt. ungreased baking dish set on a rack.

Fill baking dish with pudding mixture and cover with plastic wrap. Cover the slow cooker lid with plastic wrap and place on slow cooker. This insures the appropriate amount of steam.

Cook on HIGH for 4 hrs.

Raisin Puff Pudding with Lemon Sauce

MRS. F. W. PATTISON, BELLEVUE, WASH.

Grease a 1½-qt. mold.

For Pudding—Coarsely chop and set aside
>   ½ cup (about 2 oz.) walnuts
Sift together and set aside
>   2 cups sifted flour
>   1 tablespoon baking powder
>   ¼ teaspoon salt
Cream until softened
>   ½ cup butter or margarine
Add gradually, creaming until fluffy after each addition
>   ¾ cup sugar
Add in thirds, beating well after each addition
>   2 eggs, well beaten
Measure
>   1 cup milk
Beating only until blended after each addition, alternately add dry ingredients in fourths, milk in thirds, to creamed mixture. Finally beat only until blended (do not overbeat).

Blend in the chopped nuts and
>   1 cup (about 5 oz.) seedless raisins
Turn batter into mold. Cover mold tightly with greased lid or tie on aluminum foil, parchment paper or 2 layers of waxed paper. Place on trivet or rack in steamer or deep kettle with tight-fitting cover. Pour boiling water into bottom of steamer (enough to continue boiling throughout entire steaming period if possible).

If necessary, quickly add more boiling water during cooking period. Tightly cover steamer; steam 1½ hrs. Keep water boiling at all times.

Remove pudding from steamer and immediately loosen edges of pudding with spatula. Unmold onto serving plate. Serve hot with sauce.

For Lemon Sauce—Sift together into a double-boiler top

¾ cup sugar
1 tablespoon flour

Add gradually, stirring constantly

1 cup boiling water

Bring rapidly to boiling over direct heat, stirring gently and constantly; cook 3 to 5 min. Remove from heat.

Vigorously stir about 3 tablespoons of the hot mixture into

2 eggs, slightly beaten

Immediately blend into mixture in double boiler. Cook over simmering water 3 to 5 min., stirring slowly and constantly to keep mixture cooking evenly.

Remove from heat and blend in

2 tablespoons butter
2½ tablespoons lemon juice
1 teaspoon grated lemon peel
(page 6)

6 to 8 servings

Raisin Puff Pudding with Lemon Sauce

Use a 1½-qt. casserole. *Do not grease.* Use a 3-qt. casserole as the steamer (see preceding introduction).

Assemble pudding in casserole. Cover with a greased lid. Put casserole in steamer, cover and COOK, rotating every 2 min., until bubbling stops and it starts to pull away from the pan sides (about 35 min.). Then test for doneness with a cake tester; it should come out clean.

For Lemon Sauce—Use a 1½-qt. casserole.

COOK to boil water (about 4 min.).

Add to sugar mixture and COOK, stirring every 1 min., until boiling (about 3 min.).

Add egg mixture and COOK, stirring every 30 sec., to thicken (about 3 min.).

OVERALL COOKING TIME: 42:00

▲ Walnut Torte

Grease bottoms of two 9-in. round layer cake pans with removable bottoms or prepare *(HCL #8)* two 9-in. round layer cake pans.

Sift together and set aside

½ cup sifted flour
½ teaspoon concentrated soluble coffee
½ teaspoon cocoa or Dutch process cocoa

Grate *(page 6)*

2½ cups (about 10 oz.) walnuts
(about 4¼ cups, grated)

Reserve ½ cup grated walnuts for the frosting.

Thoroughly blend the grated walnuts with the flour mixture; divide into four equal portions and set aside.

Combine and beat until very thick and lemon-colored

6 egg yolks
½ cup sugar

Mix gently into egg-yolk mixture

1 teaspoon grated lemon peel
(page 6)
1 teaspoon rum
½ teaspoon vanilla extract

Set egg-yolk mixture aside.

Beat until frothy

6 egg whites

Add gradually to egg whites, beating well after each addition

½ cup sugar

Beat until rounded peaks are formed and egg whites do not slide when bowl is partially inverted. Gently spread egg-yolk mixture over beaten egg whites. Spoon one portion of the flour-walnut mixture over egg mixture and gently fold *(page 7)* with a few strokes until batter is only *partially* blended. Repeat with second and then third additions of flour-walnut mixture. Spoon remaining mixture over batter and gently fold *just* until blended. *Do not overmix.* Gently turn batter into pans and spread to edges.

Bake at 350°F 25 to 30 min., or until torte

tests done (see cake test, *HCL #8*).

Cool *(page 11)*; remove from pans as directed.

When torte is cooled, prepare
**Butter Frosting   (HCL #8; use the
reserved walnuts)**
Frost *(HCL #8)* torte and place in refrigerator
until ready to serve.   *12 to 16 servings*

△ **Hazelnut Torte**

Follow ▲ Recipe; substitute 1½ cups (about
½ lb.) **hazelnuts** for walnuts.

Cherry Torte

Set out a deep 9-in. spring-form pan.

Blanch *(page 6)*
1 cup (about ⅓ lb.) almonds
Grate *(page 6)* ⅔ cup of the blanched almonds (about 1⅔ cups, grated); mix with
2 tablespoons fine, dry bread crumbs
Set almond-crumb mixture aside.

Toast *(page 6)* and coarsely chop the remaining almonds; mix with
2 tablespoons sugar
Reserve almond-sugar mixture for topping.

Wash, cut into halves and remove pits from
**1 lb. dark sweet cherries (about
2¼ cups, pitted)**
Drain cherries and set aside.

Beat until very thick and lemon-colored
6 egg yolks
3 tablespoons sugar
3 tablespoons lemon juice
Set egg-yolk mixture aside.

Beat until frothy
6 egg whites
Add gradually to egg whites, beating well after
each addition
3 tablespoons sugar
Beat until rounded peaks are formed and egg
whites do not slide when bowl is partially inverted. Gently spread egg-yolk mixture over

beaten egg whites. Spoon one fourth of the
grated almond-crumb mixture over egg yolks.
Gently fold *(page 7)* with a few strokes until
batter is only *partially* blended. Repeat with
second and then third additions of almond-
crumb mixture. Spoon remaining mixture
over batter and gently fold *just* until blended.
Do not overmix. Gently turn batter into pan
and spread to edges. Place cherries evenly
over top of batter.

Bake at 350°F 30 to 40 min., or until torte
tests done (see cake test, *HCL #8*).

Set torte onto cooling rack. Cool in pan 15
min. Remove the rim from the bottom of the
pan and, if desired, cut away torte from pan
bottom and return torte to cooling rack. When
torte is completely cooled, set on baking sheet.

For Meringue—Beat until frothy
3 egg whites
Add gradually to egg whites, beating well after
each addition
6 tablespoons sugar
Beat until rounded peaks are formed.

Completely cover sides and top of torte with
the meringue. Sprinkle the reserved almond-
sugar mixture evenly over top of the meringue.

Bake at 350°F 10 to 15 min., or until meringue
is delicately browned.

Cool torte and transfer to a cake plate. Before
cutting each serving of torte, dip knife blade
into hot water. When necessary, wipe meringue from knife blade.   *12 to 16 servings*

Meringue Topped
Chocolate Cake
MRS. HARRY HAMILTON
EAST AURORA, N. Y.

Prepare *(HCL #8)* three 8-in. round layer
cake pans.

For Cake—Melt *(page 7)* and set aside
2 sq. (2 oz.) chocolate

Split into halves and set aside

⅓ cup (about 2 oz.) blanched almonds (page 6)

Sift together and set aside

1 cup sifted flour
2 teaspoons baking powder
½ teaspoon salt

Cream together until shortening is softened

½ cup shortening
1 teaspoon vanilla extract

Add gradually, creaming until fluffy after each addition

½ cup sugar

Add in thirds, beating well after each addition

4 egg yolks, well beaten

Stir in the cooled chocolate.

Measure

6 tablespoons milk

Mixing until well blended after each addition, alternately add dry ingredients and milk to creamed mixture, beginning and ending with dry ingredients.

Turn batter into pans, spreading to edges.

Beat until frothy

4 egg whites

Add gradually, beating well after each addition

¾ cup sugar

Beat until rounded peaks are formed and egg whites do not slide when bowl is partially inverted. Fold in *(page 7)*

½ teaspoon almond extract

Spread one third of meringue over batter in each pan. Sprinkle almond halves over only one layer.

Bake at 325°F about 20 min., or until meringue is golden brown.

Cool cake layers in pans on cooling racks.

After cooling, loosen sides with a spatula. Remove one cake layer, without almonds, from pan and peel off waxed paper. Place, meringue side up, onto a serving plate. Spread one half of filling over cake layer. Remove second layer, without almonds, from pan, and

place, meringue side up, on top of filling. Spread remaining filling over cake layer. Repeat with third layer and place meringue-almond side up, over filling.

For Filling—Melt *(page 7)* and set aside

2½ sq. (2½ oz.) chocolate

Mix together in top of double boiler

1 cup sifted confectioners' sugar
1 tablespoon cornstarch
⅛ teaspoon salt

Stir in and blend well

¼ cup milk

Stirring gently and constantly bring mixture rapidly to boiling over direct heat and cook 3 min. Set over simmering water; cover and cook 10 to 12 min., stirring three or four times. Remove from heat. Stir in the chocolate and

½ teaspoon vanilla extract

Cover and cool slightly, stirring occasionally.

About 12 servings

▲ Baked Alaska

Set refrigerator control at coldest operating temperature and chill a 2-qt. mold. Cover a baking sheet with two sheets heavy paper or set out a wooden board.

Line chilled mold with

Chocolate Ice Cream (one-third recipe, page 43 ; or use 1 qt. commercial ice cream)

Pack ice cream firmly against sides of mold. Fill center of mold, packing firmly, with

Strawberry Ice Cream (one-third recipe, page 45 , or 1 qt. commercial ice cream)

Place in freezing compartment of refrigerator until very firm.

Meanwhile, prepare and cool

Pound Cake (HCL #8; see note for round or square Alaska)

Split cake into two layers and trim one layer about ½ in. larger than mold. (Remainder of cake may be frosted, sliced and used as dessert.) Place cake slice on baking sheet or wooden board. Set aside.

Prepare meringue by beating until frothy
   5 egg whites
   ½ teaspoon vanilla extract
   ¼ teaspoon salt
Add gradually, beating well after each addition
   ¾ cup sugar
Beat until rounded peaks are formed and egg whites do not slide when the bowl is partially inverted.

Quickly but carefully unmold ice cream. To unmold, loosen top edge of mold with a knife. Wet a clean towel in hot water and wring it almost dry. Invert mold onto center of cake. Wrap hot towel around mold for a few seconds only. (If mold does not loosen, repeat.) Working quickly, completely cover ice cream and cake with meringue, spreading evenly and being careful to completely seal bottom edge. With spatula, quickly swirl meringue into an attractive design and if desired garnish with
   Maraschino cherries
Place in 450°F oven for 4 to 5 min., or until meringue is lightly browned.

Using two broad spatulas, quickly slide Baked Alaska onto a chilled serving plate. Slice and serve immediately.   *12 to 16 servings*

Note: **Sponge cake** may also be used as a base for Baked Alaska.

△ Baked Alaska Loaf

Follow ▲ Recipe. Substitute a 1-qt. **brick** of **commercial ice cream** for molded ice cream. Prepare **Pound Cake** (loaf, *HCL #8*) or substitute purchased oblong pound cake. Slice ½-in. layer from bottom of cake and cut layer about ½ in. larger than length and width of brick of ice cream to be used.

Peach Dumplings
JEANNE COLFLASH, DELAWARE, OHIO

Set out a 13x9½x2-in. baking pan.

Prepare (do not roll)
   Pastry for Two-Crust Pie   *(HCL #7)*
Set aside in refrigerator until ready to use.

Coarsely chop and set aside
   ¼ cup (about 1 oz.) pecans
Mix in a 1-qt. saucepan
   1 cup water
   ¾ cup sugar
   ½ teaspoon cinnamon
   ¼ teaspoon nutmeg
Stir over low heat until sugar is dissolved. Increase heat to medium and bring mixture to boiling.

Remove from heat and blend in
   3 tablespoons butter
Stir in the chopped pecans. Set sirup aside.

Rinse and plunge into boiling water to help loosen the skins
   6 medium-size (about 1½ lbs.) firm, ripe peaches
Plunge peaches into cold water. Gently slip off skins. Cut peaches into halves; remove and discard pits.

Roll pastry into an 18x12 in. rectangle about ⅛ in. thick. With sharp knife or pastry wheel cut into six 6-in. squares. For each dumpling, place a peach half, cut side up, in center of a pastry square. Fill hollow with about 1 tablespoon of a mixture of
   6 tablespoons sugar
   2 teaspoons cinnamon
   ½ teaspoon nutmeg
Top with second peach half, cut side down.

Set out
   2 tablespoons butter
Top each peach with about 1 teaspoon of the butter.

Carefully draw one corner of pastry up over peach top. Moisten edge with water. Overlap with opposite corner of pastry and press edges

PLAIN WRAP™ and
Ralphs exclusi

Is a third alternative for your food shopping needs. This "no frills" line offers you substantial savings where it counts—with your food budget.

Our "Plain Wrap ™" family is growing. Ralphs offers over 40 "Plain Wrap ™" food and household products from coffee, canned vegetables and peanut butter to laundry and dish detergents, paper towels and napkins. Is there more? Ralphs "Plain Wrap ™" family will continue to grow, Ralphs just recently introduced "Plain Wrap ™" liquor items such as vodka and gin at super savings for you.

Ralphs is proud to be the first to offer you this alternative in food shopping. And, just like everything else Ralphs sells, your complete satisfaction is guaranteed or your money will be cheerfully refunded.

Ralphs
The **_Super_** market

vings from Ralphs

Super Coupon Sa

ther
ive...

BARTLET PEARS

ORANGE DRINK

COFFEE
ALL PURPOSE GROUND

TOMATO SAUCE

together. Repeat for two remaining corners. Place each dumpling in baking pan. Pour sirup around dumplings.

Bake at 375°F 30 min. Remove from oven; brush dumplings lightly with

2 tablespoons cream

Bake 10 min. longer or until lightly browned.

Serve warm with **cream.** *6 servings*

Grandma's Apple Jack Dessert

MRS. HOWARD J. LEECH
LONGVIEW, WASH.

Prepare and bake

Deep-Dish Apple Pie *(HCL #7,*
use Pastry Topping; omit orange
juice and grated orange peel)

Cut into individual servings and turn into sauce dishes, pastry side down.

Pour warm Nutmeg Sauce over each serving.

For Nutmeg Sauce—Measure

1½ cups milk

Scald *(page 7)* 1 cup of the milk in the top of a double boiler; reserve remainder.

Mix in a saucepan

½ cup sugar
2 tablespoons flour
½ teaspoon nutmeg

Blend in the reserved ½ cup milk; add gradually, stirring constantly, the scalded milk. Bring rapidly to boiling over direct heat, stirring gently and constantly; cook 3 min. Remove from heat.

Wash double-boiler top to remove scum.

Pour mixture into double-boiler top and place over simmering water. Cover and cook about 5 to 7 min., stirring occasionally.

Remove from simmering water and blend in

1½ tablespoons butter or margarine
1 teaspoon vanilla extract

6 to 8 servings

Pineapple-Orange Fantasies

MRS. VERNON SHEAN, ROCK ISLAND, ILL.

An inspired combination of orange-flavored pastry and a piquant filling, layered into little towers that are topped with a fluff of meringue, make this prize-winner a truly original and distinguished dessert.

For Pineapple-Orange Filling—Cut into short lengths and set aside

¾ cup (3 oz.) moist, shredded
coconut

Drain (reserving sirup in a 1-cup measuring cup for liquids) contents of

1 9-oz. can crushed pineapple
(about ¾ cup, drained)

Sift together into top of a double boiler

6 tablespoons flour
⅓ cup sugar

Mix with the reserved pineapple sirup

Cold water (enough to make
½ cup liquid)

Add gradually, stirring into flour mixture with

½ cup orange juice
2 teaspoons lemon juice

Bring mixture rapidly to boiling over direct heat, stirring gently and constantly; cook 3 min. Place over simmering water. Cover and cook 5 to 7 min., stirring three or four times.

Vigorously stir about 3 tablespoons hot mixture into

2 egg yolks, slightly beaten

Immediately blend into mixture in double boiler. Cook over simmering water 3 to 5 min., stirring slowly and constantly to keep mixture cooking evenly. Remove from simmering water and blend in the coconut, crushed pineapple and

2 tablespoons butter

Cover and cool slightly, stirring occasionally. Put filling into refrigerator while preparing Orange Pastry.

For Orange Pastry—Set out baking sheets. Sift together into a bowl

1½ cups sifted flour
½ teaspoon salt

Cut in with pastry blender or two knives until pieces are size of small peas

**½ cup hydrogenated vegetable short-
ening or all-purpose shortening**

Blend in with a fork

**2 teaspoons grated orange peel
(page 6)**

Sprinkle gradually over mixture, a teaspoon at a time, about

2½ tablespoons cold water

Mix lightly with fork after each addition. Add only enough water to hold pastry together. Work quickly; do not overhandle. Shape into a ball. Divide into halves. Flatten one half at a time on a lightly floured surface. Roll from center to edge into a round about ⅛ in. thick.

With knife or spatula, loosen pastry from surface wherever sticking occurs; lift pastry slightly and sprinkle flour underneath. Cut with lightly floured 2½-in. round cookie cutter. With spatula, gently lift pastry rounds onto baking sheets.

Bake at 400°F 10 min., or until golden brown.

Carefully remove pastry rounds to cooling racks and set aside to cool.

Meanwhile, prepare Meringue.

For Meringue—Beat until frothy

2 egg whites

Add gradually, beating well after each addition

¼ cup sugar

Continue beating until rounded peaks are formed and egg whites do not slide when bowl is partially inverted. Fold in

½ teaspoon lemon juice

To Assemble Fantasies—Using three Orange Pastry rounds for each serving, spread Pineapple-Orange Filling over two rounds. Spread the third round with meringue. Cover one frosted round with the other and top with the meringue-topped round.

Bake at 400°F 3 to 4 min., or until meringue is delicately browned.

Cool and serve. *About 1 doz. desserts*

Magic Coconut Nests and ice cream

Magic Coconut Nests

Butter six 2½-in. muffin-pan wells.

Cook in top of double boiler, stirring frequently, over rapidly boiling water

**⅔ cup sweetened condensed milk
1 sq. (1 oz.) chocolate**

When mixture is thick (about 10 min.), turn into a large bowl. Stir in

1 teaspoon vanilla extract

Add and blend well

2 cups (8 oz.) moist, shredded coconut

Place about ¼ cup of mixture in each muffin well. Pack firmly around bottom and sides, letting mixture extend ½ in. above rim.

Bake at 350°F about 20 min., or until top edges are firm.

Loosen edges and lift carefully from pans. Place on cooling rack to cool.

Just before serving, fill nests with

Vanilla ice cream

6 servings

Magic Coconut Nests

Use pleated muffin papers inserted in custard cups and a small casserole.

In small casserole, COOK milk and chocolate, stirring every 30 sec., until thick (about 3 min.).

COOK nests, rotating every 1 min., until top

edges are firm (about 8 min.).

Let cool, then peel off muffing papers.

OVERALL COOKING TIME: 11:00

▲ Cream Puffs

A coffee duet—cream puffs with a mocha glaze and an elegant coffee-whipped-cream filling.

For Cream Puffs or Choux Paste—Bring to a rolling boil

> 1 cup hot water
> ½ cup butter
> 1 tablespoon sugar
> ½ teaspoon salt

Add, all at one time

> 1 cup sifted flour

Beat vigorously with a wooden spoon until mixture leaves sides of pan and forms a smooth ball. Remove from heat. Quickly beat in, one at a time, beating until smooth after each addition

> **4 eggs**

Continue beating until thick and smooth.

Dough may be shaped and baked at once, or wrapped in waxed paper and stored in refrigerator overnight.   *1 doz. large or 4 doz. miniature puffs or éclairs*

For Coffee-Glazed Cream Puffs—Form small puffs. Force dough through a pastry bag

Cream Puffs: Beat mixture with wooden spoon until it leaves sides of saucepan and forms a ball.

or drop by tablespoonfuls 2 in. apart onto lightly greased baking sheet. Bake at 450°F 15 min. Reduce heat to 350°F; bake 5 min. longer, or until golden in color. Remove to racks to cool. To serve, cut off tops and fill shells with **Coffee** or **Mocha Whipped Cream** *(HCL #8)*. Replace tops and frost with Coffee Glaze.

For Coffee Glaze—Measure into a bowl

> **3¾ cups sifted confectioners' sugar**

Add and mix thoroughly

> **¼ cup plus 2 tablespoons warm triple-
> strength coffee beverage   *(page 7)***
> **1½ teaspoons rum extract**

For Gourmet Cream Puffs—Form and bake large puffs. Increase baking time at 350°F to 20 to 25 min. Fill shells with **Sweetened Whipped Cream** (three times recipe, *HCL #8*). Replace tops, pressing down gently until ruffles of whipped cream are formed. Frost with **Chocolate Glaze** *(page 36)*.

△ Éclairs

Follow ▲ Recipe for Cream Puffs, forming dough into 4½x1-in. oblongs. When cool, cut small opening at one end and force filling through a pastry bag and a No. 6 decorating tube into éclair. Fill with **Creamy Vanilla Filling** *(HCL #8)*. Frost with Coffee or Chocolate Glaze.

Drop dough by tablespoonfuls onto a lightly greased baking sheet. Allow room for expansion.

For Chocolate Glaze (cooked)—Melt *(page 7)* 2 sq. (2 oz.) **chocolate.** Mix in heavy saucepan with 1½ cups sifted **confectioners' sugar,** 2 teaspoons **dark corn sirup,** 2 tablespoons **cream,** 1 tablespoon plus 1 teaspoon **boiling water** and 2 teaspoons **butter.** Place over low heat and stir constantly until butter melts. Remove from heat and add 1 teaspoon **vanilla extract.** Cool slightly.

For Chocolate Glaze (uncooked)—Melt *(page 7)* 3 sq. (3 oz.) **chocolate.** Blend 3 cups **confectioners' sugar** into 2 **egg whites.** Add the chocolate and 1½ teaspoons **vanilla extract.** Mix until smooth.

Savoy Meringues

Heaped with ice cream, fruit or cream filling, these snowy meringues make an elegant dessert.

Line a baking sheet with unglazed paper.

Beat until frothy
    2 egg whites
Add and beat slightly
    1 teaspoon vanilla extract
    ½ teaspoon cream of tartar
    ¼ teaspoon salt
Add gradually, beating well after each addition
    ½ cup sugar
Beat until stiff (but not dry) peaks are formed and egg whites do not slide when bowl is partially inverted.

Savoy Meringues

Drop 6 large or 18 small mounds from spoon onto baking sheet, allowing 2 in. between mounds. Using back of spoon, form meringue into shells or nests.

Sprinkle over meringue shells
    Sifted confectioners' sugar (about
    ½ teaspoon each for larger shells)
Bake at 250°F about 1 hr., or until meringue is dry to touch. (The oven door of some ranges may have to be propped open partially to maintain low temperature.) With a spatula carefully remove meringues at once and turn upside down onto same paperlined pan. (If meringues are difficult to remove from paper, raise paper from baking sheet. Lightly moisten underside of paper directly under each meringue; carefully remove shells at once with a spatula. Re-line baking sheet with dry paper.)

Return to oven 5 min. to complete drying. Cool completely on cooling rack. Meringues should be crisp, dry, and very fine textured. (Store meringues in an air-tight container so that they will not absorb moisture and soften.)

Prepare filling for
    Lemon Cream Pie or Lime Cream
    Pie (HCL #7)
Fill meringue shells with the filling. Top with
    Fresh, ripe strawberries
    About 6 large or 18 small meringue shells

▲ Blancmange

Set out
    2 cups milk
Scald *(page 7)* in top of double boiler 1½ cups of the milk; reserve remainder.

Meanwhile, sift together into a saucepan
    ⅓ cup sugar
    3 tablespoons cornstarch
    ⅛ teaspoon salt
Blend in the reserved milk; gradually add the scalded milk, stirring constantly. Bring rapidly to boiling over direct heat, stirring gently and constantly; cook 3 min. Remove from heat.

Wash double-boiler top to remove scum.

Pour mixture into double-boiler top; set over simmering water. Cover and cook about 12 min., stirring three or four times.

Lightly oil a 1-qt. mold with salad or cooking oil (not olive oil); set aside to drain.

Remove cornstarch mixture from simmering water. Cool slightly.

Beat until rounded peaks are formed
4 egg whites
Blend into cornstarch mixture
1 teaspoon vanilla extract
Spread beaten egg whites over mixture and fold *(page 7)* together. Turn into prepared mold and chill until firm.

When ready to serve, unmold onto chilled serving plate. Serve with
Fresh Strawberry Sauce (HCL #4)
4 to 6 servings

⚠ Coconut Blancmange

Follow ▲ Recipe. Blend in 1 cup finely chopped, moist shredded **coconut** with vanilla extract.

⚠ Fruit Blancmange

Follow ▲ Recipe. Blend in 1 cup well-drained, canned or sweetened fresh **fruit** with vanilla extract.

Trifle

Set out a shallow 2-qt. casserole. Chill a small bowl and rotary beater in refrigerator.

Cut into 1-in. pieces
Day-old pound cake (enough to line bottom of casserole)
Arrange over bottom of casserole. Pour over
½ cup brandy or rum
Cover and set aside.

Pour into a small cup or custard cup
¼ cup cold water

Blancmange

Sprinkle evenly over cold water
1 tablespoon (1 env.) unflavored gelatin
Let stand 5 min. to soften.

Meanwhile, scald *(page 7)* in the top of a double boiler
1½ cups milk
Beat slightly
5 egg yolks
Blend in
¼ cup sugar
Add gradually and blend in the scalded milk.

Wash double-boiler top to remove scum.

Return mixture to double-boiler top. Cook over simmering water, stirring constantly and rapidly until mixture coats a silver spoon.

Remove from heat and immediately stir in softened gelatin until gelatin is completely dissolved. Cool; chill *(page 6)* until mixture begins to gel (gets slightly thicker).

When gelatin mixture is of desired consistency, prepare whipped cream. Using the chilled bowl and beater, beat until cream is of medium consistency (piles softly)
¼ cup chilled whipping cream
Set in refrigerator while beating egg whites.

Using clean beater, beat until frothy
3 egg whites
Add gradually, beating well after each addition
¼ cup sugar
Beat until rounded peaks are formed.

Trifle

Spread egg whites and whipped cream over gelatin mixture and gently fold *(page 7)* together. Turn into the casserole. Chill in refrigerator until firm.

When ready to serve, garnish (see photo) with
> **Candied cherry**
> **Slivered blanched almonds**
> **Pieces of angelica**

Prepare
> **Sweetened Whipped Cream (one-half recipe, HCL #8)**

Force through pastry bag and No. 27 star decorating tube, forming a border around Trifle. *About 12 servings*

Trifle

Use a 1½-qt. casserole.

COOK to scald milk (about 5 min.).

Blend egg-sugar mixture into milk. Strain into clean casserole.

COOK, stirring every 1 min., to thicken slightly (about 5 min.).

OVERALL COOKING TIME: 10:00

▲ Apple-Butter Refrigerator Roll
ELBERT LUNA, AVA, MO.

Put a bowl and a rotary beater into refrigerator to chill.

Set out
> **27 vanilla wafers**

Coarsely chop
> **½ cup (about 2 oz.) walnuts**

Set aside.

Using chilled bowl and beater, whip *(page 7)*
> **1 cup chilled whipping cream**

Gently but thoroughly blend into the cream
> **⅔ cup apple butter**

Spread a thin layer on each wafer.

In a large shallow pan or dish, turn wafers on end and press together to form one long roll made up of alternate layers of wafers and whipped cream mixture. Cover outside of roll with remaining whipped cream mixture. Sprinkle with the chopped nuts.

Chill in refrigerator 3 hours. To serve, cut into diagonal slices about 1 in. thick.

8 to 10 servings

△ Brown-Edge Wafer Roll

Follow ▲ Recipe. Substitute 27 **brown-edge wafers** for vanilla wafers. Substitute **Quick Fudge Frosting** *(HCL #8)* for apple-butter and the whipped cream mixture. Omit nuts, if desired.

▲ Date-Marshmallow Dessert Roll

Chill a bowl and rotary beater in refrigerator.

Crush *(page 6)*
> **32 graham crackers (or enough to yield 2⅔ cups crumbs)**

Turn crumbs into a medium-size bowl, reserving 1 cup crumbs for topping.

Mix in
> **2 cups (about 14 oz.) pitted dates, cut in pieces** *(page 7)*
> **32 (½ lb.) marshmallows, cut in pieces**
> **¾ cup (about 3 oz.) finely chopped walnuts**
> **⅓ cup chopped maraschino cherries, well drained**

Using chilled bowl and beater, beat until cream is of medium consistency (piles softly)
> **½ cup chilled whipping cream**

Beat in with final few strokes
> **1 teaspoon vanilla extract**

Spread the whipped cream over the fruit mixture and gently fold *(page 7)* together.

Put the reserved graham-cracker crumbs onto a sheet of waxed paper. Shape the date-marshmallow mixture into a roll 14 in. long and about 2½ in. in diameter. Roll in the crumbs, coating it evenly. Wrap in waxed paper and chill in refrigerator until firm (about 12 hrs.).

To serve, cut into ¾-in. slices.

About 15 servings

△ Graham-Cracker Marshmallow Roll

MRS. G. LAMBERT, OKLAHOMA CITY, OKLA.

Follow ▲ Recipe. Do not chill bowl and beater. Reduce dates to ⅓ cup, coarsely chopped. Substitute 1½ cups (about 8 oz.) **seedless raisins** for marshmallows and cherries. Blend in 1 cup (about ½ lb.) **marshmallow cream.** Add the graham-cracker crumbs in thirds to the marshmallow-cream mixture; blend well after each addition. Omit whipping cream and vanilla. Measure ½ cup **cream** and mix in enough to hold mixture together. Do not roll in crumbs.

Chill in refrigerator 1 to 2 days.

Cherry Refrigerator Pudding

MRS. JOHN R. HITTSON

APO, SAN FRANCISCO, CALIF.

Put a bowl and a rotary beater into refrigerator to chill. Lightly butter a 9x9x2-in. pan.

Crush *(page 6)*
¾ lb. vanilla wafers (or enough to yield 3 cups crumbs)
Turn crumbs into a medium-size bowl. Using a fork or pastry blender, evenly blend with the crumbs
½ cup butter or margarine, softened
With back of spoon, firmly press one half of crumbs into an even layer on bottom of pan. Set pan aside. Reserve remaining crumbs for the topping.

Drain and set aside contents of
1 8½-oz. can pitted, sour red cherries (about 1 cup, drained)
Coarsely chop and set aside
1 cup (about 4 oz.) pecans
Cream until softened
½ cup butter
Add gradually, creaming until fluffy after each addition
½ cup sifted confectioners' sugar
Add in thirds, beating thoroughly after each addition
2 eggs, well beaten
Beat until rounded peaks are formed
2 egg whites
Spread beaten egg whites over creamed mixture and gently fold *(page 7)* together.

Turn into pan.

Add to cherries, mixing lightly
½ cup sifted confectioners' sugar
Using chilled bowl and beater, beat until cream is of medium consistency (piles softly)
½ cup chilled whipping cream
Fold cherries and pecans into whipped cream. Spread evenly over mixture in pan. Sprinkle top with reserved crumbs.

Chill thoroughly (about 4½ hrs.).

About 9 servings

Pineapple-Cheese Refrigerator Cake

MRS. L. R. SIDDERS, SHATTUCK, OKLA.

Set out a 7-in. spring-form pan.

For Crust—Crush *(page 6)*
16 graham crackers (or enough to yield 1½ cups crumbs)
Turn crumbs into a medium-size bowl. Stir in
¼ cup sugar
Add gradually, stirring in with a fork
¼ cup butter or margarine, melted
Reserve ⅓ cup crumbs for topping.

Using back of spoon, firmly press remainder of crumb mixture into an even layer on bottom of pan. Set aside.

For Filling—Empty into a medium-size bowl
1 pkg. lemon-flavored gelatin
Combine in a saucepan and heat until very hot
½ cup unsweetened pineapple juice
½ cup water
Pour the hot liquid over the gelatin and stir until gelatin is completely dissolved. Stir in
1 tablespoon lemon juice
Beat until thick and lemon-colored
3 egg yolks

Beating constantly, gradually pour the gelatin mixture into the egg yolks.

Beat until fluffy
8 oz. cream cheese, softened
Add, mixing until well blended
½ cup drained, crushed pineapple
Add gradually, beating constantly, the gelatin mixture to the cream-cheese mixture.

Chill *(page 6)* until mixture begins to gel (gets slightly thicker).

When gelatin is of desired consistency, beat until frothy
3 egg whites
⅛ teaspoon salt
Add gradually, beating well after each addition
¼ cup sugar
Continue beating until rounded peaks are formed. Spread beaten egg whites over thickened gelatin mixture and gently fold *(page 7)* together.

Turn into pan. Sprinkle reserved crumbs over top. Place in refrigerator for 10 to 12 hrs., or until firm.

Carefully run a spatula around inside of pan to loosen cake. Remove sides of pan. Do not remove cake from bottom of pan.
12 to 14 servings

Apricot Snow
CAROLYN E. STEPHENSON
WOLFE CITY, TEXAS

Pour into a small bowl
½ cup cold water

Sprinkle evenly over cold water
1½ tablespoons (1½ env.) unflavored gelatin
Let stand about 5 min. to soften.

Heat until very hot
1 cup water
Remove from heat and immediately stir in softened gelatin, stirring until gelatin is completely dissolved. Add and stir until sugar is dissolved
1 cup sugar
¾ cup apricot nectar
2 tablespoons lemon juice
¼ teaspoon salt
Cool mixture; chill *(page 6)* until mixture is slightly thicker than consistency of thick, unbeaten egg white.

Lightly oil a 2-qt. mold with salad or cooking oil (not olive oil); set aside to drain.

When mixture is of desired consistency, add
3 egg whites
Beat with electric mixer or rotary beater until mixture is very thick and piles softly (about 14 min.). Turn into the prepared mold. Chill in refrigerator until firm (about 4½ hrs.).

When ready to serve, unmold *(page 6)* onto chilled serving plate. *8 to 10 servings*

Frozen Apricot Whip
MRS. A. E. SEASTROM, HOPEDALE, MASS.

Set refrigerator control at coldest operating temperature. Put two bowls and a rotary beater into refrigerator to chill.

Prepare
Cooked Apricots (one-third recipe, page 13)
When apricots are tender, drain well and force through a sieve or food mill. Stir into apricots
1⅓ cups sugar
Let mixture stand about 15 min.

Blend into apricot mixture
1⅓ cups milk
Pour mixture into refrigerator tray; place in

freezing compartment of refrigerator until mixture is mush-like in consistency.

Using chilled bowl and beater, beat until cream is of medium consistency (piles softly)
    1 cup chilled whipping cream
Set in refrigerator while beating egg whites.

Using a clean beater, beat until rounded peaks are formed
    2 egg whites
Turn mushy apricot mixture into chilled bowl and beat until smooth.

Spread whipped cream and beaten egg whites over apricot mixture and gently fold   *(page 7)* together.

Return to refrigerator tray and freeze until firm (about 5 hrs.).   *About 1½ qts. whip*

Strawberry Mousse

WILLIAM TALBERT, CHICAGO, ILL.

Set refrigerator control at coldest operating temperature. Set out a 1-qt. mold. Put a bowl and a rotary beater into refrigerator to chill.

Sort, rinse, drain and hull enough fresh, ripe strawberries to yield
    1 cup sieved strawberries (about 1 pint)
Pour into a small bowl
    ½ cup cold water
Sprinkle evenly over cold water
    1 tablespoon (1 env.) unflavored gelatin
Let stand 5 min. to soften.

Dissolve completely by placing bowl over very hot water. Stir the dissolved gelatin and blend into the sieved strawberries with
    1 cup sifted confectioners' sugar
Rinse the mold with cold water and set aside to drain.

Using the chilled bowl and beater, beat until cream is of medium consistency (piles softly)
    1 cup chilled whipping cream

Beat into whipped cream with final few strokes until blended
    ¼ cup sifted confectioners' sugar
    ¼ teaspoon vanilla extract
Stir softened gelatin and sieved strawberries and gently mix into whipped cream until mixture is thoroughly blended. Spoon into mold.

Place in freezing compartment of refrigerator until firm.   *One 1-qt. mold*

Orange Marlow

MRS. DALE HARRMANN, OSHKOSH, WIS.

Set refrigerator control at coldest operating temperature. Put a bowl and a rotary beater into refrigerator to chill.

Set over simmering water, stirring mixture occasionally until marshmallows are melted
    32 (½ lb.) marshmallows, cut in quarters *(page 7)*
    1 cup orange juice
Remove from heat, cool and put into refrigerator to chill until slightly thickened.

Using the chilled bowl and beater, beat until cream is of medium consistency (piles softly)
    1 cup chilled whipping cream
Fold   *(page 7)* whipped cream into chilled marshmallow-orange mixture. Pour into 1-qt. refrigerator tray. Place in freezing compartment of refrigerator and freeze until mixture is firm, 4 to 6 hrs.

Serve in chilled sherbet glasses.

    6 to 8 servings

Orange Marlow

Use a 1½-qt. casserole.

Combine orange juice and marshmallows and

COOK, stirring every 1 min., to melt marshmallows (about 5 min.).

    OVERALL COOKING TIME: 5:00

Nesselrode Pudding

AMY S. BOYD, LAKE CHARLES, LA.

American version of a European creation.

Set out a 9½x5¼x2¾-in. loaf pan. Set refrigerator control at coldest operating temperature. Put a medium-size bowl and a rotary beater into refrigerator to chill.

Set out
> **1½ doz. ladyfingers (or use sponge cake cut in 4x1½x1-in. pieces)**

Line sides of the loaf pan with the ladyfingers and set aside.

Put into a large bowl and beat until very thick and lemon-colored
> **2 egg yolks**

Add gradually, beating well after each addition
> **½ cup sugar**

Add gradually, beating constantly
> **¼ cup (2 oz.) sherry**

Set egg-yolk mixture aside.

Beat until rounded peaks are formed
> **2 egg whites**

Spread beaten egg whites over egg-yolk mixture and gently fold *(page 7)* together.

Meanwhile, using chilled bowl and beater, beat until cream is of medium consistency (piles softly)
> **1¾ cups chilled whipping cream (beat only half of this amount at a time)**

Beat into whipping cream, with final few strokes until blended
> **¼ cup sifted confectioners' sugar**
> **1 teaspoon vanilla extract**

Gently fold together the whipped cream, the egg-yolk mixture and contents of
> **1 10-oz. jar (about 1¼ cups)**
> **Nesselrode mixture**

Turn the mixture into the prepared pan.

Place in freezing compartment of refrigerator until firm (about 12 hrs.).

If desired, garnish with **nuts, maraschino cherries** and **whipped cream.**

8 to 10 servings

▲ Favorite Vanilla Ice Cream

These ice cream recipes may be prepared in a dasher-type freezer or in refrigerator.

If using the dasher-type freezer, wash and scald cover, container and dasher of a 2-qt. ice-cream freezer. Chill before using.

If using a refrigerator, set control at coldest operating temperature, and chill a large bowl and a rotary beater and refrigerator trays.

Scald *(page 7)* in top of double boiler
> **2 cups milk**

Combine and then gradually stir into milk
> **1 cup sugar**
> **1 tablespoon sifted flour**
> **¼ teaspoon salt**

Stirring constantly, cook over direct heat 5 min. Remove from heat and vigorously stir about 3 tablespoons of hot mixture into
> **3 egg yolks, slightly beaten**

Immediately stir into hot mixture in top of double boiler. Return to heat and cook over simmering water 10 min., stirring constantly until mixture coats a silver spoon. Remove from heat and cool. Stir in
> **2 cups cream**
> **2 teaspoons vanilla extract**

Chill in refrigerator.

For Dasher-Type Freezer—Fill chilled container two-thirds full with ice-cream mixture. Cover tightly. Set into freezer tub. (For electric freezer, follow manufacturer's directions.) Fill tub with alternate layers of
> **8 parts crushed ice**
> **1 part rock salt**

Turn handle slowly 5 min. Turn rapidly until handle becomes difficult to turn (about 15 min.), adding ice and salt as necessary. Carefully wipe cover and remove dasher. Pack down ice cream and cover with waxed paper. Replace cover; fill dasher opening with cork.

Repack freezer in ice using
> **4 parts crushed ice**
> **1 part rock salt**

Cover with paper or cloth. Let ripen 2 to 3 hrs.

Beat with chilled beater for smooth, creamy texture. Return to refrigerator and freeze.

For Mechanical Refrigerator—Pour mixture into refrigerator trays and place in freezing compartment of refrigerator. When mixture becomes mushy, turn into chilled bowl and beat with chilled beater. This helps to form fine crystals and to give a smooth creamy mixture. Return mixture to trays and freeze until firm.   *About 1½ qts. ice cream*

Favorite Vanilla Ice Cream

Use a 1½-qt. casserole.

COOK to scald milk (about 6 min.).

Add sugar, flour and salt and COOK, stirring every 30 sec., until sugar is dissolved (about 3 min.).

Add egg yolk mixture and COOK, stirring every 30 sec., until slightly thickened and will coat a silver spoon (about 5 min.).

OVERALL COOKING TIME: 16:00

⚠ French Vanilla Ice Cream

Follow ▲ Recipe. Omit flour and increase egg yolks to 5. Substitute 2 cups **heavy cream** for cream.

French Vanilla Ice Cream

Follow 🔒 Recipe with changes as in ⚠ Recipe.

⚠ Chocolate Ice Cream

Follow ▲ Recipe. Add 2 sq. (2 oz.) **chocolate** to milk and heat until milk is scalded and chocolate is melted in top of double boiler.

Chocolate Ice Cream

Follow 🔒 Recipe with changes as in ⚠ Recipe.

⚠ Chocolate-Chip Ice Cream

Follow ▲ Recipe. Just before freezing, blend in 2 oz. **semi-sweet chocolate,** grated.

Chocolate-Chip Ice Cream

Follow 🔒 Recipe with addition as in ⚠ Recipe.

⚠ Butter-Pecan Ice Cream

Follow ▲ Recipe. Melt in a skillet 3 tablespoons **butter.** Add 1 cup (about 3¾ oz.) chopped **pecans** and heat to golden brown, occasionally moving and turning. Stir into mixture just before freezing.

Butter-Pecan Ice Cream

Follow 🔒 Recipe with additions as in ⚠ Recipe, except in browning skillet, COOK to melt butter. Add pecans and COOK, stirring every 1 min., to lightly brown (about 5 min.).

⚠ Peach Ice Cream

Follow ▲ Recipe. Substitute 1 teaspoon **almond extract** for vanilla extract. Just before freezing, blend in 1 tablespoon **lemon juice** and 1½ cups crushed fresh **peaches, sweetened.**

Peach Ice Cream

Follow 🔳 Recipe with changes as in ⚠ Recipe.

⚠ Two-Flavored Brick Ice Cream

Prepare ▲ Recipe and one-half ⚠ Recipe, using refrigerator method. Just before final freezing, form two-flavored ice cream brick by spooning alternate layers of vanilla ice cream and chocolate ice cream into refrigerator trays, starting and ending with vanilla. Return to freezing compartment until firm.

Two-Flavored Brick Ice Cream 7

Follow 🔳 Recipe with changes as in ⚠ Recipe.

Cherry-Nut Ice Cream

Set refrigerator control at coldest operating temperature. Put a small bowl and a rotary beater and a 1-qt. refrigerator tray into refrigerator to chill. Set out a double boiler.

Coarsely chop and set aside
> **2 oz. walnuts or pecans (about ½ cup, chopped)**

Rinse, drain, and remove stems and pits from
> **1½ cups fresh, dark sweet cherries**

Coarsely chop and set aside enough of the cherries to yield 1 cup chopped cherries. Reserve remaining whole cherries for garnish.

Cut into quarters *(page 7)*
> **24 (about 6 oz.) marshmallows**

Put into top of double boiler over simmering water with
> **3 tablespoons lemon juice**

Stir occasionally until the marshmallows are melted. Remove from simmering water. Stir mixture until smooth. Set aside to cool.

Blend into slightly cooled mixture
> **1 cup chilled cream or undiluted evaporated milk**

Blend in the chopped cherries, nuts, and
> **1 teaspoon grated lemon peel**
> ***(page 6)***

Using the chilled bowl and beater, beat until cream is of medium consistency (piles softly)
> **1 cup chilled whipping cream**

Turn the whipped cream onto the cherry mixture and gently fold *(page 7)* together. Pour into the chilled refrigerator tray. Place in freezing compartment of refrigerator and freeze until the mixture is mushy.

Meanwhile, chill a large bowl in refrigerator.

Turn mushy ice-cream mixture into the chilled bowl and beat until smooth. Return to refrigerator tray and freeze until firm.

Serve ice cream, garnished with the reserved whole cherries, in chilled sherbet glasses.
About 1 qt. ice cream

Cherry-Nut Ice Cream

Fresh Peach Ice Cream Superbe

Fresh Peach Ice Cream Superbe

Wash and scald cover, container and dasher of a 4-qt. ice-cream freezer. Chill thoroughly before using.

Rinse and plunge into boiling water to help loosen the skins
12 medium-size (about 3 lbs.) firm, ripe peaches

Plunge peaches into cold water. Gently slip off skins. Cut into halves; remove and discard pits. Force peaches through sieve or food mill into a bowl. Stir into peaches
2¾ cups sugar
1 tablespoon lemon juice
Let peach mixture stand 15 to 20 min.

Blend together
1½ qts. cream, chilled
1 teaspoon vanilla extract
1 teaspoon almond extract
¼ teaspoon salt
Blend into peach mixture.

Fill chilled freezer container two-thirds full with ice-cream mixture. Cover tightly. Set into freezer tub. (For electric freezer, follow manufacturer's directions.) Fill tub with alternate layers of
8 parts crushed ice
1 part rock salt
Turn handle slowly 5 min. Turn rapidly until handle becomes difficult to turn (about 15

min.), adding ice and salt as necessary. Carefully wipe cover and remove dasher. Pack down ice cream and cover with waxed paper. Replace cover; fill dasher opening with cork.

Repack freezer in ice, using
4 parts ice
1 part rock salt
Cover with heavy paper or cloth. Let ripen 2 to 3 hrs.   *About 3 qts. ice cream*

Strawberry Ice Cream
MRS. ARLAND VOGELER
WEST BROOKLYN, ILL.

A lovely pink and very pretty for a party.

Wash and scald cover, container and dasher of a 2-qt. ice-cream freezer. Chill thoroughly before using.

Thaw, according to directions. Contents of
1 16-oz. pkg. frozen strawberries (about 1⅔ cups, thawed)
Set aside.

Empty into a large bowl
1 pkg. strawberry-flavored gelatin
Add, stirring until the gelatin is completely dissolved
1 cup very hot water
Add, stirring until sugar is dissolved
1½ cups sugar
Beat until thick and piled softly
2 eggs
Blend into the beaten eggs
2 cups milk
1 cup heavy cream
1 teaspoon vanilla extract
Add egg mixture to gelatin mixture, and stir until well blended. Stir in the strawberries.

Fill freezer container two-thirds full with ice-cream mixture. Cover tightly. Place in the freezer tub. (For electric freezer, follow manufacturer's directions.) Fill tub with alternate layers of
8 parts crushed ice
1 part rock salt

▲ Ice Cream Balls

Set refrigerator control at coldest operating temperature.

Pack into deep refrigerator tray and freeze very hard
> **Favorite Vanilla Ice Cream**
> **(page 42 ; or use 1 qt. commercial vanilla ice cream)**

Crush *(page 6)*
> **24 chocolate cookies (or enough to yield 1 cup crumbs)**

Form ice cream balls with a scoop rinsed each time in hot water. Roll each ball in crumbs until thickly coated. Place balls in shallow refrigerator tray and freeze until serving time.

6 to 8 servings

⚠ Floating Snowballs

Follow ▲ Recipe. Substitute 1 cup moist shredded **coconut** for the cookie crumbs. Pour **Chocolate Miracle Sauce** (one-half recipe, *(HCL #4)* into serving dish and float coconut balls in the sauce.

⚠ Peppermint Snowballs

Follow ▲ Recipe. Substitute about 2 cups crushed **peppermint stick candy** for the cookie crumbs. Spoon **Chocolate Miracle Sauce** (one-half recipe, *HCL #4)* into serving dishes and add a peppermint ball to each.

▲ Frozen Lemon Custard

Chill until icy cold in refrigerator
> **1 cup undiluted evaporated milk**

Set refrigerator control at coldest operating temperature. Put a bowl and a rotary beater and a 1-qt. refrigerator tray into refrigerator to chill.

Beat slightly in top of double boiler
> **3 egg yolks**

Stir in
> **½ cup sugar**
> **⅓ cup lemon juice**

Cook over simmering water until mixture thickens, stirring constantly. Cool.

Stir in
> **1 teaspoon grated lemon peel** *(page 6)*

Beat until rounded peaks are formed
> **3 egg whites**

Spread the cooled lemon mixture over the egg whites and gently fold *(page 7)* together.

Beat chilled milk, using the chilled bowl and beater, until very stiff. Gently fold in egg-white mixture. Pour at once into the refrigerator tray; put tray in freezing compartment of refrigerator. Freeze until firm.

About 1 qt. frozen custard

Frozen Lemon Custard

Use a small casserole.

COOK egg yolk-sugar mixture, stirring every 1 min., until thick (about 5 min.).

OVERALL COOKING TIME: 5:00

△ Frozen Coconut Custard

Follow ▲ Recipe. Fold ½ cup (2 oz.) moist, shredded **coconut,** chopped, into custard mixture with whipped milk.

Frozen Coconut Custard

Follow **1** Recipe with addition as in △ Recipe.

Peppermint Snowballs

Grapefruit Sherbet

MRS. CAM ISAACSON, NORFOLK, NEBR.

Set refrigerator control at coldest operating temperature. Put a bowl, a rotary beater and a refrigerator tray into refrigerator to chill.

Blend together in a large bowl, in order
  1 cup sugar
  3 tablespoons lemon juice
  1 teaspoon grated lemon peel *(page 6)*
  ⅛ teaspoon salt
  1¼ cups milk

Stir until sugar is dissolved. Add gradually, stirring in
  1 cup grapefruit juice
Pour sherbet into refrigerator tray and set in freezing compartment of refrigerator. Freeze until mixture is mush-like in consistency.

Turn mixture into chilled bowl and beat with the chilled beater until smooth. Return sherbet to refrigerator tray and put in freezing compartment. Freeze until firm.

About 1½ pts. sherbet

▲ Lemon Sherbet

Set refrigerator control at coldest operating temperature. Put a bowl, a rotary beater and a refrigerator tray into refrigerator to chill.

Blend together in a large bowl, in order
  1¼ cups sugar
  ⅓ cup lemon juice
  2 teaspoons grated lemon peel
    (page 6)
  2 cups cream
Stir until sugar is dissolved. Pour into refrigerator tray and place in freezing compartment of refrigerator. Freeze until mixture is mush-like in consistency.

Turn mixture into chilled bowl and beat with chilled beater. Return sherbet to tray and put in freezing compartment. Freeze until firm.

About 1½ pts. sherbet

△ Orange Sherbet

Follow ▲ Recipe. Use only 2 tablespoons lemon juice. Add ½ cup **orange juice**. Omit lemon peel.

▲ Lime Ice

Set refrigerator control at coldest operating temperature. Chill a 1-qt. refrigerator tray.

Pour into a small cup or custard cup
  ¼ cup cold water
Sprinkle evenly over cold water
  2 teaspoons unflavored gelatin
Let stand about 5 min. to soften.

Meanwhile, heat until very hot
  3 cups water
Remove from heat and· immediately stir in softened gelatin until gelatin is completely dissolved. Add, stirring until sugar is dissolved
  2 cups sugar
Blend into gelatin mixture
  ¾ cup lime juice
  2 tablespoons lemon juice
  2 teaspoons grated lemon peel
    (page 6)
Tint to desired color by mixing in, a drop at a time
  Green food coloring (about 4 drops)
Cool. Pour into a refrigerator tray. Place in freezing compartment of refrigerator and freeze until firm (3 to 4 hrs.), stirring 2 or 3 times during freezing.

Serve in chilled sherbet glasses.

About 1 qt. ice

△ Apricot Ice

Follow ▲ Recipe. Decrease hot water to 1½ cups and sugar to 1 cup. Substitute 2 cups **apricot nectar** for lime juice and 2 tablespoons **orange juice** for lemon juice. Omit food coloring.

CANDIES and CONFECTIONS

TYPES—Candies are usually classified as two types—crystalline and noncrystalline.

Crystalline—The outstanding characteristic of standard crystalline candy is that the sugar crystals are so small that the candy at all times feels creamy and velvety to the tongue. Fondant, fudge, panocha, bonbons, pralines, nougat, divinity and kisses are common examples.

To produce great numbers of very tiny crystals and thereby ensure a creamy candy: 1) The sugar must be completely dissolved. 2) The sugar solution must be boiled to a certain temperature and then cooled to a much lower temperature before agitation or beating thereby producing a highly supersaturated solution (a solution holding more dissolved sugar than it ordinarily would at this lower temperature). 3) The sugar crystals in the supersaturated solution must recrystalize in a great number of very tiny crystals. Therefore, when the mixture has cooled to the proper temperature, it must be extensively agitated or beaten at this temperature so many small crystals may form. 4) Ingredients known as interfering substances help to avoid the formation of large crystals. In fudge, these substances are butter, corn sirup and the starch of chocolate or cocoa; in fondant, corn sirup and an acid such as lemon juice, vinegar or cream of tartar are generally used; in divinity, egg protein is the substance.

Noncrystalline—Toffee, peanut brittle, lollipops, butterscotch and caramels are examples of noncrystalline candies. As in making crystalline candies, completely dissolving the sugar crystals is important. The mixture must be cooked to a high enough temperature to produce a highly viscous solution which upon cooling quickly immediately becomes thicker or solidifies.

Ingredients which help to produce a viscous mixture in caramels are the large quantities of milk solids and fat. In caramels, the cream with corn sirup, or milk solids are classified as interfering substances and help to prevent the formation of sugar crystals. If the total amount of cream or milk is added at the beginning of cooking period of caramels, the milk or cream may curdle. Therefore, cream or milk should be added in more than one addition to avoid curdling.

During pulling of taffies, air bubbles become incorporated causing taffies to become white or, if made with molasses, become much lighter in color.

Baking soda is frequently added to brittles. It neutralizes the acidity; it also gives a porous texture to the brittle because of gas formation.

MAKE CANDY on a dry, cool day for best results. If it is necessary to make candy on a day when the humidity is high, cook the candy two degrees higher than the temperature given in the recipe.

A CANDY THERMOMETER is an accurate guide to correct stages of cooking. Test it for accuracy each time before using as the boiling point of water varies from day to day depending upon atmospheric pressure (barometric reading). Stand thermometer in boiling water (3-in. depth) for 10 minutes. It should read 212°F at sea level; if there is any variation, add or subtract the same number of degrees to or from the temperature required for the candy.

If you do not know at what degree water boils in

your community, take the average of several successive daily readings (thermometer standing in 3-in. depth of boiling water for 10 minutes). The boiling point of water drops 1°F for each 500 feet of increased altitude. Correct the temperatures given in the sirup stages in accordance with the altitude in your community.

Hang thermometer on pan so it does not touch side or bottom of pan, being certain that the bulb is covered with mixture, not just foam. Check temperature readings at eye level.

Sirup Stages and Temperatures

Thread (230°F to 234°F)—Spins 2-in. thread when allowed to drop from fork or spoon.
Soft Ball (234°F to 240°F)—Forms a soft ball in very cold water; flattens when taken from water.
Firm Ball (244°F to 248°F)—Forms a firm ball in very cold water; does not flatten in fingers.
Hard Ball (250°F to 266°F)—Forms a ball which is pliable yet hard enough to hold its shape in very cold water.
Soft Crack (270°F to 290°F)—Forms threads which are hard but not brittle in very cold water.
Hard Crack (300°F to 310°F)—Forms threads which are hard and brittle in very cold water.

THE SAUCEPAN used for cooking candy should be large enough to allow contents to boil freely without running over. The cover should be tightfitting, if cover is needed.

PREVENT GRAININESS in candy by completely dissolving all the sugar crystals; stirring and heating the sugar solution will help. If candy is stirred during cooking, stirring must stop before end of cooking period.
Cover saucepan for the first 5 minutes of boiling time, if recipe so directs. The steam formed helps to wash down any crystals that may have remained on the sides of pan.
Wash down crystals from sides of pan during cooking with a pastry brush dipped in water; move candy thermometer to one side and wash down any crystals that may have formed under thermometer.
Use clean spoons for each process—stirring, testing and beating.
Do not move, jar or stir candy during cooling period. Agitation may cause the formation of large, coarse crystals—the result a grainy, sugary candy.

Pour candy, holding saucepan within an inch or so of cooling pan or surface.
Do not scrape bottom and sides of saucepan.

STIR CANDY gently while cooking if recipe directs that candy be stirred. Move wooden spoon back and forth across bottom of pan with every few strokes.

AN ELECTRIC MIXER is better for beating divinity than beating it by hand because of the time required to beat divinity and the stiffness of the mass at the end of beating.

A MARBLE SLAB is used by professional candymakers because it has a smooth cold surface that cools candies quickly. It is easier to work large quantities of fondant and fudge on a marble slab than to beat them.

CANDIES AND CONFECTIONS IN THE MICRO-WAVE OVEN—Making candy in the microwave oven is not only quicker and cleaner than on the conventional stove, but very nearly guarantees that the final product will be smooth in texture and professional-looking in appearance. As a result, these candies make good holiday or house gifts.
Cooking Candy—Because liquids do not evaporate as readily with the microwave method as with conventional cooking, some candies must be cooked to a higher temperature than recommended in the master recipe.
Stirring is of prime importance for producing a smooth, firm candy without graininess, but we suggest a gentle hand to accompany the gentle cooking quality of the microwave method. With each recipe we note the recommended intervals for stirring and washing down crystals from the sides of the pan.
Test For Doneness—Use a candy thermometer to test these recipes. If you do not have a microwave-safe thermometer, be sure to remove the dish from the oven each time you test the temperature. If no thermometer is available, use the traditional soft ball and hard ball tests. Remember, sometimes the candy will be cooked to a higher temperature than associated with these tests.

To protect against variations in oven settings and wattage fluctuations, test the candies about every 5 min. as they near the end of the minimum recommended cooking time.

Chocolate Fudge

Butter an 8x8x2-in. pan. Set out a candy thermometer.

Put into a heavy 3-qt. saucepan
1⅓ cups milk
4 sq. (4 oz.) chocolate
Stir over low heat until chocolate is melted. Do not allow mixture to boil. Stir in
4 cups sugar
2 tablespoons white corn sirup
½ teaspoon salt
Stir over low heat until sugar is dissolved. Increase heat and bring mixture to boiling. Put candy thermometer in place. Cook, stirring occasionally to prevent scorching, until mixture reaches 234°F (soft ball stage, *page 49;* remove from heat while testing). During cooking, wash crystals *(page 49)* from sides of pan from time to time. Remove from heat.

Set aside until just cool enough to hold pan on hand. Do not jar pan or stir. When cool, add
¼ cup butter or margarine
4 teaspoons vanilla extract
Beat vigorously until mixture loses its gloss. Quickly turn into the buttered pan without scraping bottom and sides of saucepan and spread evenly. Set aside to cool.

When firm, cut into 1½-in. squares.

About 2 doz. pieces of fudge

Chocolate Fudge   1️⃣

Use a 3-qt. casserole.

COOK milk and chocolate, stirring every 1 min., to melt chocolate (about 5 min.).

Add sugar mixture and SLOWCOOK, stirring and washing down crystals every 2 min., until mixture reaches 260° or soft ball stage (about 25 min.).

OVERALL COOKING TIME: 30:00

⚠ Cocoa Fudge

Follow ▲ Recipe. Omit chocolate. Mix ¾ cup **cocoa** with sugar before adding milk.

Cocoa Fudge   2️⃣

Follow 1️⃣ Recipe with changes as in ⚠ Recipe.

⚠ Tutti-Frutti Fudge

Follow ▲ Recipe. Before turning candy into pan mix in ⅓ cup each: chopped **candied cherries pineapple and raisins.**

Tutti-Frutti Fudge   3️⃣

Follow 1️⃣ Recipe with changes as in ⚠ Recipe.

⚠ Marshmallow Fudge

Follow ▲ Recipe. Add 32 (½ lb.) **marshmallows,** cut in quarters *(page 7)*, with the butter or margarine.

Marshmallow Fudge   4️⃣

Follow 1️⃣ Recipe with changes as in ⚠ Recipe.

⚠ Peanut Butter Fudge

Follow ▲ Recipe. Substitute 6 tablespoons **peanut butter** for butter or margarine.

⚠ Pecan Fudge

Follow ▲ Recipe. Mix in 2 cups (about 8 oz.) chopped **pecans.**

Pecan Fudge   5️⃣

Follow 1️⃣ Recipe with changes as in ⚠ Recipe.

Chocolate Fudge and Hawaiian Fudge

Hawaiian Fudge

BEATRICE STOCKDALE, GOLDFIELD, IOWA

Butter an 8x8x2-in. pan. Set out a candy thermometer and a heavy 3-qt. saucepan.

Coarsely chop and set aside
   1 cup (about 4 oz.) pecans
Drain contents of
   1 14-oz. can crushed pineapple
(Reserve pineapple sirup for use in other food preparation.)

Mix in the saucepan the pineapple and
   4 cups sugar
   1 cup cream
Stir over low heat until sugar is dissolved. Increase heat and bring mixture to boiling. Put candy thermometer in place. Cook, stirring occasionally to prevent scorching, until mixture reaches 234°F (soft ball stage, *page 49;* remove from heat while testing). During cooking, wash crystals *(page 49)* from sides of pan from time to time. Remove from heat.

Set aside until just cool enough to hold pan on hand. Do not jar pan or stir. When cool, add
   2 tablespoons butter
   2 teaspoons vanilla extract
Beat vigorously until mixture loses its gloss. With a few strokes stir in the chopped pecans.

Quickly turn into the buttered pan without scraping bottom and sides of saucepan and spread evenly. Set aside to cool.

When cool, cut into 1½-in. squares.
About 2 doz. pieces of fudge

Note: For extra-smooth, mellow flavor, allow fudge to stand overnight before serving.

Hawaiian Fudge

Use a 3-qt. casserole.

COOK pineapple-sugar mixture, stirring and washing down crystals every 30 sec., until sugar dissolves (about 15 min.).

SLOWCOOK, stirring every 2 min., until mixture reaches 260° or soft ball stage (about 20 min.).
OVERALL COOKING TIME: 35:00

Chocolate Divinity

Creamy texture and smooth flavor justify the time required to make this superb candy.

Lightly butter a baking sheet. Set out a candy thermometer.

Melt *(page 7)* and set aside to cool
   2 sq. (2 oz.) chocolate
Mix together in a heavy 2-qt. saucepan having a tight-fitting cover
   2 cups sugar
   ⅔ cup water
   ½ cup white corn sirup
   ¼ teaspoon salt
Stir over low heat until sugar is dissolved. Increase heat and bring mixture to boiling. Cover saucepan and boil mixture gently 5 min. Uncover and put candy thermometer in place. Cook without stirring until mixture reaches 252°F (hard ball stage, *page 49;* remove from heat while testing). During cooking, wash crystals *(page 49)* from sides of pan from time to time.

Meanwhile, beat in a large mixer bowl until stiff (but not dry) peaks are formed

3 egg whites

When sirup reaches 252°F, immediately remove from heat and remove thermometer. Beating constantly with an electric mixer on high speed, pour the sirup in a steady stream onto the stiffly beaten egg whites (do not pour onto beaters). When mixture begins to lose its gloss, turn off motor and lift beaters. In the early stage, the mass flows down from the beaters in a continuous ribbon. Continue beating until mixture no longer flows but holds its shape (about 35 min.).

At this point, *quickly* blend in the cooled chocolate and

1 teaspoon vanilla extract

Drop by teaspoonfuls onto the baking sheet. Cool thoroughly. *About 4 doz. pieces of divinity*

Chocolate Divinity

Use a 3-qt. covered casserole.

COOK chocolate, stirring every 1 min., until melted (about 3 min.).

COOK sugar mixture, stirring every 1 min., to dissolve sugar (about 15 min.). Continue to COOK, stirring and washing down crystals every 1 min., until boiling (about 5 min.).

Cover and SLOWCOOK until mixture reaches 260° or hard ball stage (about 20 min.).

OVERALL COOKING TIME: 43:00

▲ Fondant

Set out a candy thermometer and a large platter or marble slab. (Surface must be smooth and level.)

Mix together in a heavy 3-qt. saucepan having a tight-fitting cover

3 cups sugar
1½ cups water
¼ teaspoon cream of tartar

Stir over low heat until sugar is dissolved. Increase heat and bring mixture to boiling. Cover saucepan and boil mixture gently 5

min. Uncover and put candy thermometer in place. Continue cooking without stirring. During cooking, wash crystals *(page 49)* from sides of saucepan from time to time. Cook until mixture reaches 238°F (soft ball stage, *page 49;* remove mixture from heat while testing). Remove candy thermometer.

Wipe the platter or slab with damp cloth. Immediately pour sirup onto the platter or slab; do not scrape pan. Without stirring, cool to lukewarm or until just cool enough to hold platter on hand. Pour onto cooled sirup

1 teaspoon vanilla extract

With a wide spatula or wooden spoon, work fondant in circles from edges to center until white and creamy. Pile into a mound, cover with a bowl and allow to rest 20 to 30 min.

With hands, work fondant (in a kneading motion) until soft and smooth.

Ripen at least 24 hrs. in a tightly covered jar. Shape into candies or use in following recipes.
About 1¼ lbs. fondant

▲ Bonbons

Follow ▲ Recipe. Reserve about one third of ripened fondant for dipping. Divide remainder into three or more portions. Work into one portion several drops **pistachio extract** and less than a drop of **green food coloring** (dip tip of a wooden pick into food coloring, then into fondant). In another portion use **vanilla extract** or **almond extract.** Use **rose extract** and **red food coloring** for the remainder. If adding finely chopped **nuts, coconut, candied fruits, dates, figs** or **raisins,** work in with fingers only until blended. (Use alone or in any combination.)

Shape into rolls 1 in. in diameter. Cut into small uniform pieces and shape into balls or ovals, slightly flattened on one side. Keep small; dipping increases size. Allow fondant to stand on racks or trays lined with waxed paper. Dry several hours before dipping.

When ready to dip, place reserved fondant in

top of double boiler. Melt over simmering water, stirring constantly. Heat to 130°F (no higher). Add flavoring and coloring. Dip a center to test for proper coating consistency.

Using a fork or candy dipper, lower a center, rounded side down, into fondant and cover completely with fondant. Immediately remove, scraping bonbon on edge of pan to remove excess fondant. Place flattened side down onto waxed paper. Make fancy swirl on top by twirling fork or dipper. (Dipping fondant may be reheated to maintain proper consistency.)

⚠ Fondant Patties

Follow ▲ Recipe. Fondant can be used for making patties about 1 hr. after working fondant with hands. Cover a flat surface with waxed paper or aluminum foil.

Stirring constantly, melt fondant over simmering water, heating fondant to 130°F (no higher). Add desired coloring and flavoring. If fondant is not the consistency of thick cream, thin it with **hot water,** stirring in 1 teaspoonful at a time. Pour fondant into rounds (about the size of quarters) from measuring cup or small pan having a sharp lip. (Warm measuring cup or pan with hot water and dry before filling with fondant.)

When patties are firm, arrange on edge, side-by-side, with small squares of waxed paper separating them. *About 5 doz. patties*

⚠ Peppermint Patties

Follow ⚠ Recipe. Blend into the melted fondant, a drop at a time, **red food coloring** and **peppermint extract.**

▲ Nougat Fingers

Butter a 10x6x1½-in. pan. Set out a candy thermometer and a heavy 2-qt. saucepan.

Coarsely chop and set aside
> ½ cup (about 3 oz.) blanched almonds
> **(page 6)**

Cut *(page 7)* into halves and set aside
> ½ cup (about 3 oz.) candied red
>   cherries

(If necessary, pat cherries dry between pieces of absorbent paper.)

Mix together in the saucepan
> 2½ cups sugar
> ¾ cup white corn sirup
> ½ cup water

Stir over low heat until sugar is dissolved. Increase heat and bring mixture to boiling. Cover saucepan and boil mixture gently 5 min. Uncover and put candy thermometer in place. Cook without stirring until mixture reaches 270°F (soft crack stage, *page 49;* remove from heat while testing). During cooking, wash crystals *(page 49)* from sides of saucepan from time to time.

Meanwhile, beat in a large mixer bowl until stiff (but not dry) peaks are formed
> ⅓ cup egg whites (about 3 egg whites)
> ⅛ teaspoon salt

When the sirup reaches 270°F, immediately remove from heat and remove thermometer. While bubbles are subsiding, carefully wash down crystals from pouring side of pan.

Beating constantly with an electric mixer on medium speed, pour the sirup in a steady fine stream into center of egg whites (do not pour onto beaters). Do not scrape bottom or sides of saucepan. Stop beating as soon as ingredients are well mixed.

(If a hand rotary beater must be substituted for the electric mixer, turn the beater on its side; beat mixture in spoon fashion while adding the sirup. Then turn beater upright and beat hard to thoroughly mix the sirup and egg whites.)

Stir in the almonds, cherries and
> 1 teaspoon vanilla extract
> ½ teaspoon almond extract

Beat with spoon until mixture falls in chunks from the spoon held about 12 in. above the bowl. Turn candy into the prepared pan and press down firmly and evenly with hand. Set aside on cooling rack.

When nougat is completely cool, cover pan tightly. Set aside to ripen at least 24 hrs.

Loosen sides of candy and shake well ·to remove block of candy from pan to cutting board. Cut with a sharp, long-bladed knife into pieces about 2x1 in. Wrap each piece in waxed or glassine paper.

Store in a tightly covered container in a cool, dry place.   *About 2½ doz. Nougat Fingers*

△ Nougat Centers for Caramel-Pecan Roll

Butter a 15½x10½x1-in. jelly roll pan and set out a 1-qt. saucepan having a tight-fitting cover. Prepare one-half ▲ Recipe. Substitute finely chopped **pecans** for toasted almonds; chop cherries finely. Omit almond extract.

Turn the mixture onto buttered pan and divide into two equal mounds. With buttered hands shape each mound into a roll or block about 15 in. long. Allow nougat to set a few minutes. Wrap each portion tightly in waxed paper; let stand until nougat holds its shape.

See recipe for **Caramel-Pecan Roll** (*on this page*) to complete candy.   *Two Nougat Centers*

Caramel-Pecan Roll

Prepare and set aside
  **Nougat Centers for Caramel-Pecan
  Roll (on this page)**
Butter a 15½x10½x1-in. jelly roll pan. Set out a candy thermometer and a heavy 1½-qt. saucepan. Lay out two sheets of waxed paper about 20 in. long; lay the two sheets side by side and clip lengthwise edges together.

Spread out on the waxed paper over an area the size of the jelly roll pan
  2½ cups (about 10 oz.) pecan halves
Set aside.

Set out in a warm place
  1 cup cream
  ¼ cup butter
Mix together in the saucepan
  1 cup sugar
  1 cup white corn sirup
  Few grains salt
Stir over low heat until sugar is dissolved. Increase heat and bring mixture to boiling. Put candy thermometer in place. Cook, without stirring, until mixture reaches 244°F (firm ball stage, *page 49;* remove from heat while testing). During cooking, wash crystals (*page 49)* from sides of saucepan from time to time.

Gently stir mixture and add ¼ cup of the cream so slowly that boiling will not stop. Keeping mixture boiling vigorously, add the remaining cream by tablespoonfuls. Occasionally stir mixture between additions of cream. (The addition of the cream will take about 25 min.) Stir in the butter. Cook mixture to 244°F.
Set pan on cooling rack; cool mixture to 200°F.

Remove candy thermometer. Mix in
  1½ teaspoons vanilla extract
Turn into buttered pan without scraping bottom and sides of saucepan. Let stand on a cooling rack a few minutes until caramel is just cool enough to handle quickly with the hands. (If caramel gets too cool, it will not stick to the pecans.)

Loosen the caramel from the sides of the pan; carefully turn sheet of caramel over the pecans. Carefully and gently press the caramel onto nuts.
Lay one Nougat Center at edge of caramel sheet. Roll until the nougat is coated with caramel. Cut caramel where coating meets. Form a second roll.

Wrap each caramel roll tightly in waxed paper. Set aside until firm enough to cut. To store caramel pecan rolls, wrap in waxed or glassine paper and place in a tightly covered container. Store in a cool, dry place.
    About 5 doz. pieces of candy

Chocolate Caramels Supreme

Butter an 8x8x2-in. pan. Set out a candy thermometer and a heavy 3-qt. saucepan.

Chop and set aside
⅔ cup (about 3 oz.) nuts
Melt *(page 7)* and set aside to cool
4 sq. (4 oz.) chocolate
Set out
3 cups heavy cream
2 tablespoons butter
Pour 1 cup of the cream into the saucepan and mix in
2 cups sugar
1 cup white corn sirup
¼ teaspoon salt
Stir over low heat until sugar is dissolved. Increase heat and bring mixture to boiling. Put candy thermometer in place. Cook, stirring frequently, until mixture reaches 234°F (soft ball stage, *page 49;* remove from heat while testing). During cooking, wash crystals *(page 49)* from sides of saucepan from time to time. Stirring constantly, gradually add another cup of cream to saucepan, so slowly that boiling will not stop. Continue cooking, stirring frequently, over low heat until mixture reaches 234°F. Stirring constantly, gradually add remaining cream and the butter to mixture so slowly that boiling will not stop.

Stirring frequently, cook to 244°F (firm ball stage, *page 49;* remove from heat while testing). (Consistency of the candy tested in cold water will be the consistency of the caramel. Caramel mixture cooked to 246°F will give a slightly firmer caramel than mixture cooked to 244°F.)

Remove mixture from heat and remove candy thermometer. Immediately add the melted chocolate and nuts to mixture with
1 tablespoon vanilla extract
Stir just until blended. Immediately pour hot mixture into the buttered pan. Do not scrape bottom and sides of saucepan. Set caramel mixture aside on cooling rack in a cool place.

Creamy and Cocoa Taffy

When completely cooled, (several hours or overnight) invert onto a cutting board and remove pan. Working in a cool place, mark candy into 1-in. squares; using a sharp, long-bladed knife, cut candy with a sawing motion. Wrap each caramel tightly in waxed or glassine paper. Store in a covered container in a cool, dry place. *About 5½ doz. caramels*

Note: For **Vanilla Caramels,** omit chocolate.

▲ Creamy Taffy

Butter a large, shallow pan or platter. Set out a candy thermometer.

Mix together in a heavy 2-qt. saucepan
2¼ cups sugar
1½ cups white corn sirup
4 teaspoons vinegar
¼ teaspoon salt
Stir over low heat until sugar is dissolved. Increase heat and bring to boiling, stirring constantly. Add slowly so boiling does not stop
½ cup undiluted evaporated milk
Put candy thermometer in place. Continue cooking, stirring constantly, until mixture reaches 248°F (firm ball stage, *page 49;* remove from heat while testing). During cooking, wash crystals *(page 49)* from sides of saucepan from time to time. Remove from heat and remove thermometer. Immediately pour mixture into the buttered pan without scraping bottom and sides of saucepan.

When mixture is just cool enough to handle, butter hands. Work in a cool place. Pull a small portion of the taffy at a time, using only the tips of the fingers, until candy is white in color and no longer sticky to the touch. Twist pulled strip slightly and place on waxed paper or on a board. Cut with scissors into 1-in. pieces. Wrap in waxed or glassine paper.

Store in a tightly covered container in a cool, dry place.   *About 8 doz. pieces of taffy*

Creamy Taffy

Use a 3-qt. casserole.

COOK sugar mixture, stirring and washing down crystals every 30 sec., until sugar is dissolved (about 15 min.).

Add milk and COOK, stirring every 30 sec., until boiling (about 5 min.).

SLOWCOOK, stirring and washing down crystals every 2 min., until mixture reaches 260° or firm ball stage (about 25 min.).

OVERALL COOKING TIME: 54:00

△ Cocoa Taffy

Follow ▲ Recipe. Mix ⅔ cup **Dutch process cocoa** with the sugar.

Cocoa Taffy

Follow Recipe with changes as in △ Recipe.

Salt Water Taffy

NAOMI CHILDS, TIONESTA, PA.

Butter a large, shallow pan or platter. Set out a candy thermometer.

Mix together in a heavy 2-qt. saucepan
2 cups sugar
1¼ cups white corn sirup
1 cup water

Stir over low heat until sugar is dissolved. Increase heat and bring mixture to boiling. Put candy thermometer in place. Continue cooking, stirring constantly, until mixture reaches 244°F (firm ball stage, *page 49;* remove from heat while testing). During cooking, wash crystals *(page 49)* from sides of saucepan from time to time. Remove from heat and remove thermometer. Immediately blend in
1 tablespoon butter
1½ teaspoons salt
Pour mixture into the buttered pan without scraping bottom and sides of saucepan.

When mixture is just cool enough to handle, butter hands. Work in a cool place. Pull a small portion of the taffy at a time, using only the tips of the fingers, until candy is firm and cool and no longer sticky to the touch. While pulling, work in
Food coloring
Extract
The amounts of food coloring and flavoring will depend on the amount of taffy being pulled and the color and flavor desired. Twist pulled strip slightly and place on waxed paper or on a board. Cut with scissors into 1-in. pieces. Wrap in waxed or glassine paper.

Store in a tightly covered container in a cool, dry place.   *About 6 doz. pieces of taffy*

Note: Good flavor and color combinations are **peppermint extract** and **red food coloring; wintergreen** and **green; lemon** and **yellow.** Or use **vanilla extract** and omit coloring.

Crackle Peanut Brittle

Lightly butter two baking sheets. Set out a candy thermometer.

Mix together in a heavy 3-qt. saucepan having a tight-fitting cover
2 cups sugar
1 cup white corn sirup
1 cup water
Stir over low heat until sugar is dissolved. In-

crease heat and bring mixture to boiling. Cover saucepan and boil gently 5 min. Uncover and put candy thermometer in place. Continue cooking without stirring until mixture reaches 234°F (soft ball stage, *page 49;* remove from heat while testing). During cooking, wash crystals *(page 49)* from sides of saucepan from time to time. Mix in

2 cups (about 11 oz.) raw peanuts
2 teaspoons butter

Cook over low heat, stirring frequently, until mixture reaches 300°F (hard crack stage, *page 49;* remove from heat while testing). Remove from heat and remove thermometer. Add, mixing well

2 teaspoons baking soda
1 teaspoon vanilla extract

Pour onto the baking sheets, spreading as thinly as possible. As soon as candy is cool enough to handle, wet hands in water and stretch candy as thin as desired. Turn candy over and cool completely.

When cool and firm, break candy into medium-size pieces. Store in tightly covered container.

About 2 lbs. peanut brittle

Crackle Peanut Brittle

COOK sugar mixture, stirring every 2 min., until melted and then until boiling (about 5 min.). Cover and continue to COOK, scraping crystals from sides until all are dissolved (about 5 min.).

Uncover and COOK, stirring and washing down crystals every 2 min., until mixture reaches 234° or soft ball stage (about 20 min.).

Add peanuts and butter and COOK, stirring every 2 min., until mixture reaches 300° or forms hard, brittle threads (about 15 min.).

OVERALL COOKING TIME: 45:00

Butterscotch

ESTHER E. BRUCKER, WHEATON, ILL.

A rich butterscotch that "melts in your mouth."

Butter an 8x8x2-in. pan. Set out a candy thermometer.

Mix together in a heavy 2-qt. saucepan

1 cup sugar
½ cup butter
¼ cup molasses
2 tablespoons water

Stir over low heat until sugar is dissolved. Increase heat and bring mixture to boiling.

Put candy thermometer in place. Cook, stirring constantly, until mixture reaches 300°F (hard crack stage, *page 49;* remove from heat while testing). During cooking, wash crystals *(page 49)* from sides of pan from time to time.

Remove from heat and remove thermometer.

Pour sirup into the buttered pan without scraping bottom and sides of saucepan. Mark candy quickly into squares with a sharp knife before it cools. Set aside to cool.

When hard, break candy into pieces. Store in tightly covered container in cool, dry place.

About ¾ lb. Butterscotch

Butterscotch

Use a 2-qt. casserole.

COOK sugar mixture, stirring every 30 sec., until dissolved (about 10 min.).

SLOWCOOK, stirring and washing down crystals every 2 min., until mixture reaches 310° or forms hard, brittle threads (about 25 min.).

OVERALL COOKING TIME: 35:00

Toffee

Butter an 8x8x2-in. pan. Set out a candy thermometer.

Chop very finely and set aside
1½ cups (about 6 oz.) pecans

Melt in a heavy 2-qt. saucepan

1 cup butter

Add, stirring constantly until well blended
1 cup sugar
3 tablespoons water

Put candy thermometer in place. Stirring occasionally to prevent scorching, cook until mixture reaches 300°F (hard crack stage, *page 49;* remove from heat while testing). Remove from heat and remove thermometer.

Blend in
1 teaspoon vanilla extract
Quickly turn into the buttered pan and spread to corners. Immediately mark the candy into squares with a sharp knife. Set aside to cool.

Partially melt over simmering water, being careful not to overheat
½ lb. milk chocolate
Remove chocolate from simmering water and stir until completely melted. Set aside to cool.

When candy is cool, spread with one half of the melted chocolate. Sprinkle half of the chopped nuts over the chocolate. Invert pan onto a piece of waxed paper and remove pan. Cover with remaining chocolate and nuts. Set aside on cooling rack in a cool place.

When candy is hard, break into pieces. Store in a tightly covered container between layers of waxed paper, aluminum foil or moisture-vapor-proof material. Texture improves after several days.   *About 1½ lbs. Toffee*

Pecan Pralines

Pralines are a Creole candy. French colonists in New Orleans adapted them from an old French recipe, substituting native American pecans for the almonds of France.

Set out a heavy 2-qt. saucepan and a candy thermometer. Line baking sheets with aluminum foil or greased waxed paper.

Pecan Pralines

Measure
2 tablespoons butter
1½ cups (about 6 oz.) pecan halves
Set aside.

Mix together in the saucepan
1 cup firmly packed dark brown sugar
1 cup granulated sugar
½ cup cream
Stir over low heat until sugar is dissolved. Increase heat and bring mixture to boiling. Put candy thermometer in place. Cook without stirring until mixture reaches 230°F (thread stage, *page 49;* remove from heat while testing). During cooking, wash crystals *(page 49)* from sides of pan from time to time.

Stir in the butter and pecan halves.

Continue cooking, stirring occasionally to prevent scorching, until mixture reaches 234°F (soft ball stage, *page 49;* remove from heat while testing).

Remove from heat and remove thermometer. Cool mixture 2 to 3 min. without stirring. Gently stir mixture for about 2 min., or until it becomes slightly thicker and pecans appear well coated with sugar mixture. Quickly drop by tablespoonfuls onto the aluminum foil or greased waxed paper. The candy will flatten. Allow to stand until cool.

When completely cooled, wrap each praline in

waxed or glassine paper. Store in a covered container in a cool, dry place.

About 1½ doz. pralines

Anise Lollipops

MRS. EDWARD M. LEE, MAPLETON, IOWA

Set out a candy thermometer and 16 to 20 small wooden skewers. Line baking sheets with aluminum foil or greased waxed paper.

Mix together in a heavy 2-qt. saucepan having a tight-fitting cover

2 cups sugar
⅔ cup white corn sirup
½ cup water

Stir over low heat until sugar is dissolved. Increase heat and bring mixture to boiling. Cover saucepan and boil mixture gently 5 min. Uncover and put candy thermometer in place. Continue cooking without stirring. During cooking, wash crystals *(page 49)* from sides of saucepan from time to time. Cook until mixture reaches 300°F (hard crack stage, *page 49;* remove from heat while testing). Remove from heat and remove thermometer.

Add and stir in just to mix

¼ teaspoon anise oil
8 to 10 drops red food coloring

Quickly pour sirup into small rounds on the aluminum foil or waxed paper. The sirup will flatten out. Press a wooden skewer into each lollipop immediately. Allow to cool slightly. Remove from foil or waxed paper before lollipops are completely cooled.

When cool, wrap each lollipop in waxed or glassine paper. Store in covered container in a cool, dry place. *About 1½ doz. 3-in. lollipops*

Anise Lollipops

Use a 3-qt. casserole.

COOK sugar mixture, stirring every 30 sec., to dissolve sugar (about 15 min.). Cover and continue to COOK until boiling (about 3 min.).

Uncover and SLOWCOOK, stirring and washing down crystals every 2 min., until mixture reaches 310° or forms hard, brittle threads (about 25 min.).

OVERALL COOKING TIME: 43:00

Candied Delights

Lightly butter an 8x8x2-in. pan. Set out a heavy 2-qt. saucepan.

Pour into a small bowl

1 cup cold water

Sprinkle evenly over cold water

4 tablespoons (4 env.) unflavored gelatin

Let stand about 5 min. to soften.

Meanwhile, mix together in the saucepan

3 cups sugar
½ cup hot water

Stir over low heat until sugar is dissolved. Increase heat and bring mixture to boiling. Cook rapidly for 10 min. without stirring. During cooking, wash crystals *(page 49)* from sides of saucepan from time to time.

Stir in softened gelatin, stirring until gelatin is completely dissolved. Simmer the mixture

Candied Delights

10 min. longer, stirring occasionally. Remove from heat. Stir in

¾ cup (1 6-oz. can) frozen orange juice concentrate (do not add water)

Pour mixture into prepared pan; cool.

Chill in refrigerator about 6 hrs.

Cut into 1-in. squares with a sharp knife and roll squares in

Sifted confectioners' sugar

Set in refrigerator until ready to serve.

About 5½ doz. pieces of candy

Candied Delights

Use a 3-qt. casserole.

COOK sugar and water, stirring every 1 min., until boiling and sugar is dissolved (about 15 min.).

Add gelatin and continue to COOK without stirring, until mixture starts to thicken (about 5 min.). SLOWCOOK, stirring every 2 min., until very thick (about 15 min.).

OVERALL COOKING TIME: 35:00

Coffee Truffle Balls

Set out

⅓ cup butter

10 oz. milk chocolate

Grate *(page 6)* 2 oz. of the chocolate (about ¾ cup, grated). Mix with the grated chocolate

1½ teaspoons concentrated soluble coffee

Set aside in refrigerator.

Place remaining chocolate in the top of a double boiler with

¼ cup heavy cream

Heat over simmering water, stirring occasionally, until chocolate is melted. Remove from simmering water and cool slightly.

Divide the butter into small pieces and stir into the melted chocolate until butter is melted. Add and mix in thoroughly

½ teaspoon concentrated soluble coffee

Chill thoroughly in freezing compartment of refrigerator about 1 hr., or until firm.

When mixture is chilled, spoon about 1 teaspoonful at a time onto the reserved chocolate-coffee mixture. Quickly work with fingers to form a ball and to coat with the chocolate.

About 1½ doz. truffle balls

Coffee Truffle Balls

Use a 1½-qt. casserole.

COOK chocolate and cream, stirring every 30 sec., to melt chocolate (about 6 min.).

OVERALL COOKING TIME: 6:00

Caramel Popcorn Balls

For Popped Corn—If using an electric popper, follow the manufacturer's directions. Otherwise, for each pan of corn, melt in heavy skillet or saucepan having a tight-fitting cover

1 tablespoon hydrogenated vegetable shortening, all-purpose shortening, lard or cooking oil

Add enough popcorn (about ¼ cup) to just cover bottom of skillet and cover tightly. Shake pan over medium heat until popping stops. Turn corn into a large bowl. Set aside to keep warm. In the same way prepare

3 qts. popped corn

Caramel Popcorn Balls

For Sirup—Measure and set aside

⅓ cup undiluted evaporated milk

Mix together in a saucepan

1 cup firmly packed brown sugar

¾ cup white corn sirup

2 teaspoons vinegar

¼ teaspoon salt

Stir over low heat until sugar is dissolved. Increase heat and bring mixture rapidly to boiling without stirring. Put candy thermometer in place. Cook until mixture reaches 280°F, (soft crack stage, *page 49;* remove from heat while testing). During cooking, wash crystals *(page 49)* from sides of pan from time to time.

When temperature has reached 280°F, add the evaporated milk gradually (so that mixture does not stop boiling), while stirring constantly. Bring caramel mixture to 280°F again, stirring constantly. Remove from heat and remove thermometer. Stir in

1 teaspoon vanilla extract

For Popcorn Balls—Gradually pour hot caramel sirup into center of warm popped corn. With long-handled fork, *quickly* blend to coat corn with sirup. Dot corn with

2 tablespoons butter or margarine

With buttered hands, gather and press into firm balls.   *About 1½ doz. 3-in. popcorn balls*

Caramel Popcorn Balls

Use a 1½-qt. casserole.

COOK sugar mixture, stirring and washing down crystals every 1 min., to boil and dissolve sugar (about 10 min.). Continue to COOK until mixture reaches 280° or soft crack stage (about 15 min.).

Add milk as directed and COOK, stirring every 1 min., to return to 280° (about 5 min.).

OVERALL COOKING TIME: 30:00

Spiced Nuts

Set out a candy thermometer and a double boiler having a cover. Lay out on a flat surface a long piece of waxed paper.

Set out

4 cups (about 1 lb.) nuts (such as walnuts or pecans)

Mix together in a large bowl and set aside

¼ cup sugar

2 tablespoons cinnamon

½ teaspoon cloves

½ teaspoon nutmeg

½ teaspoon ginger

Mix together in the top of the double boiler

1 cup sugar

¼ cup water

2 tablespoons cinnamon

½ teaspoon cloves

½ teaspoon nutmeg

½ teaspoon ginger

Stir over low heat until sugar is dissolved. Increase heat and bring mixture to boiling. Cover and boil mixture gently for 5 min. Uncover and put candy thermometer in place. Continue cooking without stirring until mixture reaches 238°F (soft ball stage, *page 49;* remove from heat while testing). During cooking, wash crystals *(page 49)* from sides of pan from time to time.

Remove thermometer and place double-boiler top over simmering water. Immediately add the nuts and mix until well coated with the sirup. Turn into the reserved sugar mixture in the bowl. Toss lightly until all nuts are well coated. Turn onto the waxed paper and separate the nuts. Set aside to cool completely.

Store in a tightly covered container in a cool, dry place.   *About 4 cups Spiced Nuts*

Spiced Nuts

Use a 3-qt. covered casserole.

COOK sugar-water mixture, stirring every 1 min., to boil and dissolve sugar (about 10 min.).

Cover and continue to COOK, scraping crystals from sides and bottom every 1 min., until all crystals are dissolved (about 3 min.).

Uncover and COOK, stirring and scraping every 1 min., until mixture reaches 238° or soft ball stage (about 15 min.).

OVERALL COOKING TIME: 28:00

▲ Caramel-Nut Mallows

Line a baking sheet with waxed paper.

Put into the top of a double boiler

½ lb. vanilla caramels

3 tablespoons hot water

Heat over simmering water, stirring frequently, until caramels are melted.

Meanwhile, finely chop

¾ cup (about 3 oz.) pecans

Set out

32 (½ lb.) marshmallows

Using a fork, dip each marshmallow into the melted caramel and turn until well coated. Roll in the chopped nuts. Place on the waxed paper. Set in a cool place until caramel is firm.

Store in a covered container in a cool, dry place.   *32 pieces of candy*

△ Coconut-Chocolate Mallows

Follow ▲ Recipe. Substitute 6 oz. **semi-sweet candymaking chocolate for dipping** for the caramels and water. Partially melt chocolate over simmering water, being careful not to overheat. Remove chocolate from heat and stir until completely melted. Blend in ½ teaspoon **vanilla extract.** Substitute **Toasted Coconut** (double recipe, *HCL #7)* for the nuts.